Education in Change

Education in Change

REPORT OF THE CURRICULUM REVIEW GROUP

New Zealand Post-Primary Teachers' Association

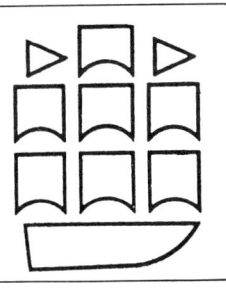

LONGMAN PAUL LIMITED

LONGMAN PAUL LIMITED
5 Milford Road, Auckland

© Post-Primary Teachers' Association

This book is copyright. Apart from any fair dealing
for the purpose of private study, research, criticism
or review, as permitted under the Copyright Act, no
part may be reproduced by any process without written
permission. Enquiries should be made to the publisher.

First published 1969
Reprinted *1970

SBN 582 68770 5

Printed in Hong Kong by
Dai Nippon Printing Co (International) Ltd

Contents

ACKNOWLEDGEMENTS, *vi*

CURRICULUM REVIEW GROUP, *vii*

FOREWORD BY SIR JOHN NEWSOM, *ix*

PREFACE, *xi*

INTRODUCTION, *xiii*

1 A Basis for Judgement, 1
2 The Nature of Change in Society, 2
   SUMMARY: THE CHALLENGES OF CHANGE, 8
3 A Pattern of Values, 10
   SUMMARY: HUMAN VALUES AND SCHOOL PRACTICE, 22
4 Learning and Enquiry, 26
   SUMMARY: COGNITIVE OBJECTIVES, 38
5 The Measurement of Objectives, 40
   SUMMARY: EVALUATION OF GROWTH, 54
6 The Curriculum, 57
   SUMMARY: THE BALANCED CURRICULUM, 71
7 Interaction between School and Community, 74
   SUMMARY: NEW COMMUNICATIONS, 78

CONCLUSION, 80

NOTES, 81

BIBLIOGRAPHY, 104

INDEX, 108

Acknowledgements

The committee gladly takes this opportunity to express its indebtedness to several people. MRS P. MEIKLE, Executive Editor of LONGMAN PAUL, has given invaluable help and advice during the final editing of the report while MR W. R. HALLIBURTON of New Plymouth Boys' High School cheerfully carried the editorial burden of the early drafts. MR O. L. GILMORE, Principal of the Secondary Teachers' College, Auckland, has kindly allowed the committee to use the college facilities for all its meetings. THE NZPPTA EXECUTIVE have supported the work at all times, and the successive presidents, the late MR J. S. WEBSTER, MR A. H. SCOTNEY and MR C. B. NEWENHAM, have done everything to give the committee confidence in the value of its work. Many other people have contributed useful advice and written submissions. The members of the committee are particularly grateful to those who presented papers on the curriculum in April 1968. We are indebted to the following for permission to use copyright material; Department of Education, Wellington, New Zealand, 1968 for an extract from *Science for Form 5;* Harcourt Brace & World, Inc., 1965, for extracts from *Science Teaching and Testing* by Leo Nedelsky; Harvard University Press, 1966 for extracts from *Toward a Theory of Instruction* by Jerome S. Bruner; Rand McNally, 1964, for an extract from *Handbook of Research on Teaching,* B. S. Bloom, N. L. Gage, ed.; and Teachers' College Press, Teachers' College, Columbia University, 1962, for an extract from an article in *Curriculum Crossroads* by Arthur W. Foshay. David McKay Co. Inc., 1964, for an extract from *Taxonomy of Educational Objectives,* Handbook II, B. S. Bloom, D. R. Krathwohl and B. B. Masia.

The Curriculum Review Group N.Z.P.P.T.A.

MR P. W. BOAG	N.Z.P.P.T.A., WELLINGTON
MR T. C. EDMONDS	HERETAUNGA COLLEGE
MR H. E. FLYNN	SECONDARY TEACHERS' COLLEGE, AUCKLAND
MR J. A. GALE	AUCKLAND TEACHERS' COLLEGE
MR P. E. HOLMES	WAIHEKE DISTRICT HIGH SCHOOL
MR D. T. HUNT	GLENDOWIE COLLEGE
MR B. A. HUNTER	PAPATOETOE HIGH SCHOOL
MR H. M. HUNTER	BELMONT INTERMEDIATE SCHOOL
MR J. G. JOHNSON	OTARA COLLEGE
MR J. R. KELLY	WAIHI COLLEGE
MR O. W. G. LEWIS	SELWYN COLLEGE
DR R. J. MCBEATH	UNIVERSITY OF HAWAII
DR A. H. MCNAUGHTON	UNIVERSITY OF AUCKLAND
MR J. P. MILLAR	AUCKLAND GRAMMAR SCHOOL
DR W. J. D. MINOGUE	UNIVERSITY OF AUCKLAND
MR R. G. MUNRO (CHAIRMAN)	SECONDARY TEACHERS' COLLEGE, AUCKLAND
MISS H. M. RYBURN	WESTLAKE GIRLS' HIGH SCHOOL
MR A. H. SCOTNEY	RONGOTAI COLLEGE
MR B. P. F. SMITH	SECONDARY TEACHERS' COLLEGE, AUCKLAND
DR W. B. SUTCH	WELLINGTON

Foreword
BY SIR JOHN NEWSOM

I count it a signal honour to contribute a brief Foreword to this important Report, but I suppose the justification is that I have spent nearly six years as Chairman or Vice-Chairman of an English Central Advisory Council for Education which dealt with similar problems to those which faced Mr Munro and his colleagues. Someone once said that original thought was a waste of time because everything wise had already been written but, sadly, even if this proposition was true, the harsh fact is that much of what is written about education is quite unreadable and, even if understood, has had precious little effect on events. This Report is an exception to the common experience; it is brief and to the point, it is obviously the work of those with class-room experience, it stresses that the art and science of teaching requires a definition of aims based on adequate research and statistical material.

The genesis of the Report was 'the concern many teachers felt at the lack of adequate criteria by which to judge changes in the curriculum and teaching practice', and its purpose could be compressed into two quotations: firstly 'to understand better the ways in which children can grow, and more especially to understand how the kind of education they receive can help or hinder growth', and secondly, 'to make an unprejudiced exploration of the growth of children and to direct attention to fresh ways of looking at their growth.'

Perhaps the most significant conclusions can, again, be given in three direct quotations:

Firstly . . . 'that the future of education depends on change which is firmly based on the findings of imaginative experimentation and research.'

Secondly . . . 'Many of our present difficulties may arise . . . because public and schools alike have not rethought in the context of the contemporary world, our traditional ideas of what constitutes "a good education".'

Thirdly . . . 'A good education is one in which the highest value is placed on: "the urge to enquire, concern for others, the desire for self-respect".'

To me, perhaps the most important thing about the Report, apart from its content, is that a group of educationists have been given not only the blessing of the New Zealand Post-Primary Teachers' Association but, from the same source, the finance to make the

Report possible. In too many countries Teachers' Associations tend to be identified with causes that are not strictly educational; that cannot be said about this one.

In the past too many of us have believed that we were competent teachers by some 'hunch' or by purely pragmatic experience. We did not really know what our objective was nor did we know very much, if anything, about the way children actually acquire skills and knowledge. This Report gets the priorities right: it defines the purpose, it describes the learning process and it suggests methods by which the purpose can be achieved by practising teachers. Above all it is mercifully brief, free from the jargon which bedevils so much educational writing throughout the world, and of real practical help to secondary teachers. I hope it has a wide circulation in New Zealand—and farther afield.

John Newsom

Preface

The secondary school teachers of New Zealand have over recent years come increasingly to examine the work of our schools, and in particular to question whether in this era of universal secondary education the work they are doing is still the most appropriate.

This concern was most clearly expressed at the Annual Conference of the New Zealand Post-Primary Teachers' Association in August 1966, the second conference in succession to spend considerable time debating amendments to the School Certificate examination. The delegates resolved that the Association should give priority to a study of the work of the schools before any further attempts were made to design the perfect system for examining that work. The Association's Executive was instructed to initiate such an examination of the objectives of the New Zealand secondary school system. This was a task which had been attempted previously in this country only by the 1942 Thomas Committee and then only in the limited context of the implications for the secondary school curriculum of the removal to the sixth form of the University Entrance examination. The conference decision recognised not only the existence of this significant omission in our educational development but also the responsibility that rests on the teachers themselves to examine and, as far as possible, to chart for the next few decades the course of the system of which they are an integral part.

For the purpose of this study the Executive set up a special committee as widely representative as possible—the Curriculum Review Group—and wisely selected its chairman Mr R. G. Munro, a lecturer at the Auckland Secondary Teachers' College and at that time a member of the Association's National Executive. This was a choice that has been more than justified by the inspiration, application and integrity which Mr Munro has brought to his task. The Association deeply appreciates his work and indeed the work of the whole group. This volume is ample evidence of their deep concern for the ultimate objectives of education and with the growth of the individual. It is a provocative statement which will, I hope, inspire each individual teacher to examine his own philosophy of education. If it can do that, it has more than justified the effort that has been put into it.

The group has left one major question practically untouched—the training of the teachers needed to attain the selected objectives. Full examination of this closely related topic may well provide the material for a further volume.

This is a report prepared by New Zealand teachers following examination of the New Zealand situation. Most of the problems dealt with, however, are universal, and I commend the report to teachers and parents everywhere as a serious contribution to educational discussion. I am confident that it will be found to be an exciting and stimulating document.

                                                          C. B. NEWENHAM

President
N.Z. POST-PRIMARY TEACHERS' ASSOCIATION

January 1969
WELLINGTON, NEW ZEALAND

Introduction

This report is about young people. Its purpose is to enquire into the quality of their growth in our secondary schools. If the report provokes public debate about the fundamental ends and processes of education, it will have fulfilled its authors' purposes.

The enquiry reported on here arose out of the concern many teachers felt at the lack of adequate criteria by which to judge changes in the curriculum and teaching practice. When the committee began its work early in 1967 it had first to search for satisfactory criteria that would be acceptable to all its members: an exacting task which took six months of open informal debate. The consensus statement arrived at forms Section 1 of the report, 'A Basis for Judgement'.

Throughout the report the value of various educational practices has been estimated in relation to two principal questions:

1. Are these practices consistent with the over-arching educational aims accepted by the committee?
2. Do they reflect what is known about the processes of child growth?

The educational aims accepted by the committee naturally depended on the attitudes and purposes its members brought with them. But, in order to gain enough knowledge of child growth and the learning process, the committee had to explore the findings of research. It was well served here. Papers contributed in many fields enabled members to form their opinions against a background of world enquiry. Through its explorations the committee came to believe that the future of education depends on change which is firmly based on the findings of imaginative experimentation and research. In studying such findings, the committee was furthering the basically practical aim of its work: namely to understand better the ways in which children can grow, and more especially to understand how the kind of education they receive can help or hinder growth. The report is therefore essentially pragmatic in its approach to education.

The committee also came to believe that persons who are concerned for education must look beyond the present serious difficulties and try to see clearly what kinds of educational change are desirable —the direction in which we want education to move in New Zealand. Many of our present difficulties may arise, the committee feels, because public and schools alike have not rethought in the context of the contemporary world, our traditional ideas of what constitutes 'a good education'.

In the past education has most often been thought of as a narrow form of 'training' which children accepted in the hope of obtaining specific material rewards. Today many people are beginning to see that education is much more than that: it forms a major part of the process of individual and social growth and should be self-motivating because its rewards are inherent. This report is directed towards the development of a concept of self-motivated learning.

The notes to this report make a substantial contribution to its argument; they and the text make up a whole. Readers are therefore urged to read text and notes together.

[1] A Basis for Judgement

Because the committee's thinking about major educational aims is closely related to its view of the nature of human growth, this statement of major aims consists of a short list of human qualities which education should be concerned to promote at all times. The highest value is placed on:

> the urge to enquire;
> concern for others;
> the desire for self-respect.

The Urge to Enquire

The impulse to enquire is an innate one. It leads man to sharpen and deepen his awareness and to search for new meanings in his life and environment; and it leads him to rich and diverse ways of looking at himself and the universe.

Concern for Others

Concern for the welfare of other human beings implies a feeling of personal responsibility towards society. Christianity and some other religions express this concern in the doctrine of love; the humanist expresses it in respect for the right of other people to realise their full potential—a respect which requires the individual both to govern his own actions so that they do not impede the growth of others, and actively to help others to grow. The human being who is concerned for others does all he can to increase their self-respect.

The Desire for Self-Respect

Self-respect depends on the individual's view of himself, on his capacity to develop his abilities and insights to the fullest extent, and on his desire to reflect deeply on the nature and effects of his behaviour.

Throughout the report the committee has sought to establish educational positions which will help to develop these human qualities in young people.

[2] The Nature of Change in Society

As enquiry progressed it became clear that an assessment of present trends in our society should precede any detailed discussion of educational goals. Some attempt had to be made to predict, on the basis of such an assessment, the salient features of our society in the next few decades, particularly those that are likely to do most to shape the needs of young people.

AGENTS OF CHANGE

1. The World Society

'The world has shrunk.' 'The nations of the world must work together or perish.' Statements like these have become commonplaces. But they are commonplaces whose tremendous implications are too seldom carried at the front of our minds, too seldom affect the policies of governments or the attitudes of influential persons; and are more seldom still reflected in educational systems.

Modern means of transport and communication have made forever impossible the national isolation of past ages; modern weapons have made all wars people's wars. They have made a world that is interdependent to an extent never before known; a world in which international co-operation is already a necessary condition for survival, and the creation of a genuinely global society a necessary aim. If governments and people in influential positions too often fail to see these needs, increasing numbers of young people are impatiently aware of them. An informed and critical adolescent opinion is beginning to emerge which distrusts nationalist policies and the politicians who make them. Many young men and women are trying—some of them through organisations such as Volunteer Service Abroad—to help bring into being a unified and co-operative world society in which young people of every race and colour can feel they 'belong'.

We must hope that our education system will encourage more young people to explore ways of contributing to the growth of a world society which alone can assure them of a future and so give point and direction to their lives.

2. Economic Need

Today New Zealand's income from primary exports is insufficient to maintain our living standards at the high level of the past twenty years. If we wish for a widely prosperous, Western-type society we must not only increase our efficiency in the production and marketing of primary produce but also establish high-quality manufactures. To do these things we must develop the skills of our population to the fullest extent. Trainees today need enough flexibility of mind to learn new skills and adapt to new conditions. Young people in our schools will need this flexibility even more so that they can readily undertake the retraining and re-education they will require during their working lives—perhaps more than once—in order to fit them for jobs not yet invented.

If young people are to be able to respond confidently to the challenges of new complex technologies they must be prepared to stay at school longer. Those who will work to develop new New Zealand industries must not only acquire exacting skills, they must also be capable of inventing new skills and new products to enable New Zealand to participate in world markets. Only an education system sensitive to the need to develop the innate creativity of young people can satisfy this demand for inventive minds.

We are a small nation. We need these minds in large numbers and cannot afford to waste the potential ability and enterprise of even one young New Zealander. We must therefore combat the tendency of many young people to leave school too early and enter jobs without a future because the starting pay is good. We must in particular encourage far more girls to reach a higher level of education, because those who become mothers will do most to influence the next generation through the values and attitudes they transmit to their children. Women who are as well educated and well trained as men will be able to enter a wider range of occupations and contribute more to our country's economic growth. Above all we must do far more to give equality of educational opportunities to all types of children by providing curricula which suit their needs and give them opportunities for enjoyment and success. We waste many of our human resources when we fail to involve large numbers of our children in worth-while learning.

The quality of our economic growth depends on the quality of our people. If we recognise that education is concerned with all aspects of human growth, if we encourage our schools to seek for varied and better ways of learning so that young people can grow to the limits of their capacity, we shall have the strongest basis for national economic growth.

3. The Movement of Economic and Ethnic Groups

Fast and efficient transport and communications, together with opportunities in new industries, are making family movement steadily more attractive. Unfortunately, the financial advantages of moving a family are often accompanied by difficulties of adjustment for children, particularly where the continuity of their learning is broken. It is possible that fewer children would suffer if the curriculum placed a greater emphasis on ways of enquiring and less on remembering. In schools which valued enquiry-skills children would have less difficulty in adjusting to new programmes (*see below* pp. 28–39 for a discussion of enquiry-skills).

Where large numbers of young families have been attracted into urban housing estates and new towns, their children also experience serious difficulties outside the schools. The new communities lack social coherence and young people often find it impossible to attain a sense of identity. Perhaps regional industrial development is needed so that migrating populations become part of existing communities and thus quickly gain a sense of belonging. In the short-term, however, special efforts should be made by schools and educational authorities to design curricula which will help young people in the new communities to attain a sense of purpose.

Many teachers feel a special concern for the education of Maori and Pacific Island children, particularly those whose parents have migrated to the cities. Yet in spite of widespread debate on the needs of these children the full implications for curriculum development have still to be identified. Certainly if we are to help these children we must obtain a thorough understanding of their cultural values and a knowledge of the thought-forms they bring into the classroom. It has also been suggested that their early learning should be as much concerned with non-verbal as with verbal activities so that full advantage can be taken of their ability to express themselves in dance, music and role-playing. However, the difficulty of educating these children is basic and will not be overcome cheaply; we shall need highly skilled curriculum planning, research and teacher training if we are to avoid creating under-privileged racial groups.

4. The Family

Few institutions in our society are changing more rapidly than the family. Changes in the functions of its members, changes in values, changes in patterns of social behaviour are all influencing the family and its effectiveness as a social and educative unit.

Perhaps the new role of women in our society is responsible for the most dramatic changes in family life. Far fewer women than formerly accept the role of wife and mother as sufficient for completeness in their lives, and increasing numbers are entering employment which affords them additional opportunities for satisfaction and independence. Some families have adjusted to having working mothers and established new patterns of responsibility, particularly for the care of young children, but others have failed to do so and their children are being deprived of a secure upbringing.

The survival of the family as an effective social unit obviously depends on the general acceptance of the values it is expected to preserve and nurture. Conscious care and mutual concern have often been cited as necessary aspects of family life, and yet it is these values which are in jeopardy in our modern society. Their erosion is illustrated in our present attitude to the aged: family groups increasingly avoid responsibility for their care and thrust it on to local authorities. It is not surprising, therefore, that young people should tend to under-value the old (and also to under-value the importance of helping others to attain self-respect).

'Parents are failing to transmit values to the young' is a charge easily laid; and it is sometimes true. Yet should we wonder that, in a society in which all familiar beliefs are being questioned, the middle-aged are confused and uncertain? The breakdown in the transmission of positive values is a corporate social issue and cannot be attributed to one group alone. No doubt some parents are too passive in their concern for their children, but there are many others who are struggling to revalue our changing society and offer their children positive guidance.

In the past the churches complemented and reinforced the family by handing on a stable pattern of values and many people continue to expect them to fulfil this function. But the role of the churches is now more limited. Whether they can re-establish their influence on our community values remains an open question, especially as many people are either indifferent to them or even hostile. But, in spite of their weakened position, many churches are working positively to define values appropriate to our time and to experiment with ways of communicating with young people.

This report is particularly concerned with the contribution the schools can make to the development of desirable values in young people. Can the schools help pupils to evaluate our society and aid them in their search for security in change? Some parents seem to think so, or at least they are prepared to leave the responsibility to the schools. If teachers can help young people to recognise the need for responsible and co-operative behaviour and encourage them to discuss changes in society and consider the implications for their future, the schools will indeed fulfil an important function. But their responsibilities can never be total. Without the concerted and committed efforts of all groups in the community, their efforts will fail to make a significant impact on their pupils.

5. Adolescents

It should not surprise us that today's environment has led to some changes in the behaviour of adolescents. Press, radio and television have focused on their foibles, and commercial interests have cultivated them for their uncommitted income. Yet despite their new prominence and increased opportunities for making independent decisions, their pattern of behaviour is still familiar. Some have shown hostility towards the establishment but, in this country at least, most young people passively accept the *status quo*. Those who have rejected established modes of behaviour or turned to the meretricious values promoted by commerce, are in most cases insecure and unable to formulate satisfying patterns of behaviour for themselves. Again the schools could help all young people by encouraging them to question their society, to test their ideas and values in open discussion and gradually think their way through to their own social criteria.

6. Mass Media

Radio, television and pulp magazines are blamed for many of our social ills but, though they undoubtedly do affect behaviour, the dangers from them are probably more limited than we suspect. Their most unfortunate effect is on children with backgrounds of failure and poor mental health: young people who become dependent on the media and whose entire behaviour may be shaped by them. But, for most children the mass media, particularly television, offer a wide range of educational experiences not otherwise available to them.

The effects of the mass media on children depend on attitudes developed in our homes and schools and on the sense of responsibility shown by programme organisers. The special tasks of the schools are to develop critical minds capable of discrimination and to provide dependent children with greater educational success (*see below* pp. 13–14 for a discussion of success and achievement). As these children grow up, the pressure of informed public opinion should do much to raise the standard of programmes.

7. Science and Technology

Technology, capitalising on scientific thought, has given the late twentieth century unprecedented power and wealth. But this same scientific endeavour is also being applied less happily to the shaping and controlling of human behaviour. Powerful methods of analysis and prediction are used by industry, commerce and government to pre-determine people's needs, to create demands and to reduce the individual to a mere statistical cipher. Indeed control, both economic and political, now depends in part on the machines produced by the new technology. Within industry the computer could become an agent for controlling both men and machines, and in national affairs communication systems are already significantly influencing the 'closed politics' of diplomacy.

Education has an important responsibility here, not only to develop young minds flexible enough to understand the nature of science and technology, but also to prepare young people against attempts to use scientific procedures to intimidate and control them.

8. The Growth of Knowledge

Science is contributing, perhaps more than any other discipline, to the rapid growth of knowledge. But it is not alone in its responsibility for this remarkable growth: there is a continuous outpouring of research from all specialised fields of study (old and new), a 'knowledge explosion' which is forcing many people to seek new ways of ordering the vast array of information available to them. This explosion raises new questions for curriculum builders: 'Can the total of new knowledge be appreciated by a single individual?'; 'Can modern information storage systems help us to retrieve the knowledge we cannot hope to store in the memory banks of a single brain?'; 'Can a modern curriculum give children effective ways of retrieving and applying new knowledge to problem-solving situations in all aspects of their lives?' This report will attempt tentative answers to these questions; it will suggest that we may help children to order their knowledge by equipping them with a readily understandable pattern of human enquiry (*see below* pp. 33–39). Such an approach to learning could give young people the confidence to continue their education throughout their lives.

9. Educational Change

Since the publication of *The Post-Primary School Curriculum* (Thomas Report, 1942), there have been significant changes in secondary education. Today a higher proportion of children go on to secondary schools and the very large increase in sixth form numbers shows clearly they are staying there longer. The type of secondary school has also changed. Co-educational schools have become the norm rather than the exception and all schools are offering a wider range of courses than did the predominantly 'academic' schools of the 1940s.

There have been changes too in the responsibilities accepted by our schools. The needs of the less successful pupils and of those suffering from emotional disturbance are beginning to be recognised and teachers are more active than formerly in the revision of examination syllabuses. But important as these changes and revisions are, our attack on educational problems is at best piecemeal and shows little evidence of being based on any fundamental reappraisal of the present needs of young people. Too little has been achieved. A better educational system will not emerge without improved and possibly longer teacher-training, improved staffing ratios and conditions of service, new attitudes to learning and new resources, and the widespread introduction of counsellors with specialist training. A formidable catalogue of needs, but one which we cannot afford to ignore if the quality of our society is to match the requirements of this changing world.

SUMMARY OF SECTION [2]

The Challenges of Change

1. To encourage young people to explore ways of contributing to the growth of a world society which alone can assure them of a future.

2. To reassert the importance of helping others to attain self-respect.

3. To help young people to recognise the need for responsible and

co-operative behaviour, and encourage them to discuss changes in society and consider the implications for their future.

4. To develop in young people a capacity to make consistent value judgements in the face of social, political and economic pressures.

5. To recognise that national growth depends on the quality of learning in our schools.

6. To realise the potential ability and enterprise of all pupils by helping them to develop flexible and inventive minds capable of adaptation and growth in new conditions.

7. To equip young people with a readily understandable pattern of human enquiry.

8. To ensure that pupils understand the nature of science and are not intimidated or overwhelmed by it.

9. To provide highly skilled curriculum planning, research and teacher-training to help in the education of the less successful children.

[3] A Pattern of Values

To accept the intrinsic worth of all human beings, to respect their right to hold their own opinions and make their own decisions, and to feel responsible for one's own actions and those of others are the marks of a mature person. The members of the committee see the development of maturity of this kind as a basic aim of education.

SCHOOL PRACTICES AND MATURITY

There is little doubt that the learning environment we provide in our schools has a significant effect on the values developed by pupils. If we wish them to develop certain qualities we must therefore make sure that our teaching practices embody these qualities. Present practices should be examined in terms of the attitudes and values they encourage; if these attitudes prove undesirable we should seek for new practices that create opportunities for growth towards maturity. The committee believes that to create such opportunities our schools must have growth as a central aim.

Mature behaviour cannot be imposed from outside. It must become valued and be developed through practice. Young people need civilising experiences, both in and out of the classroom, to help them to grow towards maturity. For example, teachers should hold open discussions which encourage social as well as intellectual growth and educational authorities should provide attractive facilities for recreation, relaxation and meals.

Motivation for Learning

The methods used to educate young people clearly reflect the social goals of an education system. In the nineteenth century, as in some classrooms even today, the desire to learn was generated by fear of punishment. Coercion was accepted as a classroom practice and rationalised by schools on the grounds that, to maintain good order, they must suppress children's innate waywardness. This approach to schooling is still advocated by some members of our community, but it is inconsistent with our present understanding of children's capacity for self-motivated growth and the undesirable results of the use of force.[1] If we wish to produce assured, self-respecting young people, capable of independent growth, we must begin by respecting them as individuals. A teacher's manner towards his pupils should show the same courtesy he expects to receive from them. A teacher who dominates or bullies young people and determines their actions by arbitrary and inflexible restrictions cannot expect them to see value in co-operative behaviour.

In so far as teachers in the past have relied mainly on external forms of motivation, such as fear of failure and punishment, they have tended to do things *to* children, to educate by direct instruction, with the result that they have given their pupils little opportunity to make genuine choices. More recently there have been attempts to humanise this process by designing 'child-centred' curricula which help teachers to do things *for* children by carefully predigesting the learning expected of them: workbooks which ask pupils to fill in the blanks are examples of teaching devices used in this type of curriculum. These attempts too, although well-intentioned, do little to develop in children a capacity to make decisions for themselves. Young people are simply led by more humane procedures to accept the will of the teacher and become dependent on him.

Educationists, aware of the limitations of both direct instruction and 'child-centred' approaches, have searched for fresh ways of motivating children which will help them to develop self-respect and independence of mind.[2] Experiments during the last half-century have investigated the importance of intrinsic motivation in children—motivation arising from the curiosity of the children themselves and their interest and involvement in what they are doing. The development of this intrinsic desire to learn seems to depend on the extent to which children are respected by their teachers. If they can see that their initial attempts to learn are valued, they will more readily find satisfaction in their work. Children whose desire to learn is associated with delight in their growing competence may well continue to enjoy learning throughout their lives and to value thoughtful actions at all times.[3]

If mutual respect is a desirable basis for classroom activity, the implications are clear: in order to allow children the freedom necessary to develop initiative and self-respect teachers must be prepared to do things *with* children rather than *to* them or *for* them. Moreover, the teacher who wishes to release this independent drive in his pupils must know a great deal about them so that he can organise their learning activities and set appropriate goals. He must know about their interests, skills, knowledge, attitudes and values before he can lead them to contribute fully to classwork and thus to participate in their own education. Much of this understanding can be obtained more readily outside the classroom in informal discussions with pupils and during other school activities. Many more opportunities should be provided for teachers to learn more about their pupils by mixing with them in small groups.

The Place of Individual Competition

Competition has long been accepted as part of our individualistic social system. But this system often forces individuals and groups to behave in a manner inconsistent with principles of mutual respect. We do not have to look far for current illustrations: the widening gulf between standards of living in the rich and poor countries is evidence enough of the essentially self-seeking nature of competitive individualism. This self-seeking may appear to be denied by charitable aid programmes, but among developing nations, aware of their meagre share of profits from foreign investment, it is still responsible for a deep distrust of affluent nations.

Many people place an absolute value on competition as the principle upon which our society is based, and fail to admit its destructive effects. Yet even in economic matters, where central importance has been claimed for competition, its validity as a principle of progress is now being challenged by economists and administrators on the grounds that it leads to wasteful duplication of effort.[4] Competitive practices abound in New Zealand, in the arts as well as in sport and business; but, if we should find, through a thorough reappraisal of their effects, that they reinforce aggressive and thoughtless behaviour, we should be prepared to reject them and search for a rationale better fitted to our social needs.

Traditionally, we have encouraged competition in our schools also, particularly in the classroom, where competition between individual pupils has been regarded as an important way of encouraging them to achieve standards of excellence. However, relatively few children—and chiefly those who are confident and successful in their school work—show marked progress in a competitive situation; and their success may be teaching them to value arrogant behaviour. The remainder, particularly children at the bottom of the rank order, experience varying degrees of failure because they bear the stigma of having fallen below the performance of the children at the top. Competition thus places artificial barriers in the way of pupil growth. Competition against the top does harm to those who are measuring themselves against an impossible mark, for it is unrealistic for all children to be set the same immediate goals. It can lead children of low initial attainment to over-strive or else to become reluctant to learn at all. In both cases there is unnecessary anxiety and consequent loss of self-respect. It is unfortunate that over-striving is often the result of pressures from parents who refuse to take a realistic view of their children's abilities.

The Rank Order

Where individual competition is made use of in the pursuit of excellence the end is often corrupted by the means. For example, the tendency to cheat that some pupils show reveals a desire to win at any cost. The drive to get to the top is seen as an objective in itself and learning becomes incidental. Some teachers are guilty of encouraging this attitude, for, instead of commending excellence in behaviour and performance, they commend the rank order as important in itself. The place figure associated with the competitive order succeeds only in comparing one child's achievement with another's, whereas a valid estimate of a child's progress can only be made against his own initial endowment and achievement.[5]

Competition and Achievement

For all children achievement is important because of the feelings of emotional well-being and security that attend it. We make a false assumption when we argue that a competitive class situation gives equal opportunities for the individual success of pupils. Those with low initial attainment, who most need praise and encouragement, tend to be those who are least likely to receive it. If a child's total growth is our most important objective, praise of his progress can only be meaningful in relation to his known ability. If achievement in relation to ability was measured and rewarded more children would enjoy worth-while encouragement.

Children, it cannot be disputed, show both readiness to compete with each other and readiness to co-operate. However, from the time they are very young, their parents and others often encourage competition at the expense of co-operation. Children bring this readiness to compete into the classroom; but teachers who understand the undesirable effects of competition do not use it to motivate children.[6] Today many educationists are rejecting competitive practices for a second reason: a growing weight of evidence suggests that all learning is enhanced in a co-operative atmosphere.[7]

The Non-Competitive Classroom

When we move away from an emphasis on the rank ordering of our pupils we acknowledge realistically their natural differences of ability; we accept the fact of relative merit and do not present children with artificial absolute goals which many of them cannot help but fall short of. By this means we also help to lessen unnecessary tensions between them.

In a non-competitive classroom, where individual contribution is valued, we can promote opportunities for diverse growth instead of setting ourselves to turn out standard products. Moreover, young people can grow by facing challenges which are relevant to their own interests and abilities and can begin to share in their own independent growth and to see it as a personal adventure. For in seeking and finding patterns of co-operation with others and competition with their own standards, they are venturing in a self-motivated fashion.

OPPORTUNITIES FOR RESPONSIBLE GROWTH

Teachers are often doubtful about their function in a classroom which gives children increased opportunities to participate in their own education. They fear that increased freedom will prevent them from establishing acceptable standards of behaviour. But children can grow in desirable ways even though their behaviour is not dictated by authority. Careful organisation and guidance in the school and classroom can give rise to patterns of co-operative behaviour which are acceptable both to young people and to their teachers. Free and self-motivated growth is not incompatible with organisation. Indeed children will gradually learn for themselves that an unorganised situation invariably reduces their freedom of action but that, if class activities are organised in such a way that opportunities and responsibilities are clearly complementary, real freedom of action becomes possible. The teacher can help children to see how responsibilities and freedom are linked: for example, he may free them during certain class periods to pursue their own enquiries on the clear understanding that they must present their findings to the class at a certain time. When children recognise that responsible action contributes to their own growth they will feel that full sense of independence which comes from having seen for oneself the value of setting voluntary restrictions on one's actions.

Children can see the signposts to acceptable behaviour in the working situations the teacher creates. For example, when a class is concerned with enquiry the skilled teacher will make sure that the children examine all points of view and in time he will bring them to value unbiased interpretations and decisions. Honesty and open-mindedness are thus placed at a premium. The teacher is not simply saying: 'These are honest and desirable attitudes', he is illustrating their advantages in working situations.

New Learning Resources

New teaching programmes are urgently needed to help teachers to build classroom environments in which pupil contribution is valued. Teachers themselves should share directly in curriculum development so that advantage can be taken of their experience and new programmes can be tested in the classroom while they are being designed. Whatever designs evolve, they will need to include specific advice and practical help towards developing a classroom climate of the kind discussed here. But though good up-to-date programmes should be available, they must not place teachers in strait-jackets; teachers must remain responsible for 'inventing' the actual classroom opportunities they offer children.

Our teachers also need new resources. In new teaching programmes throughout the world emphasis is given to pupil initiative, exploration and enquiry by means of carefully designed and tested guides which set the stage for pupil discovery. These programmes include all the necessary materials such as pupil texts, teachers' guides, programmed sequences, laboratory manuals, films, film strips, film loops, models, charts, demonstration equipment and equipment for pupil experiment. The teacher has a new role in helping to develop programmes. He also has the responsibility of standing alongside his pupils rather than in front of them, helping to lead them to the most useful ways of discovering and understanding their work for themselves. With the aid of the teaching and learning resources named above, the teacher can expect children to accept increasing responsibility for much of their classwork and, through the exercise of responsibility, to become increasingly aware of the implications of their own thoughts and actions.

In many new programmes memorising information is no longer seen as a major end in education. A determination to uncover the processes and fundamental concepts of studies has placed the 'content' of facts and drills in a new perspective. Facts emerge and become valued as part of the experience which is directed toward the understanding of basic principles and concepts.

New programmes also acknowledge the need to match classwork

to the learning readiness of children of different initial capacities. Alternative forms of many new programmes are being produced for different ability levels so that teachers can choose those appropriate to specific groups of children.[8]

Classrooms and Private Study

New courses which encourage young people to learn by discussion and enquiry require physical conditions very different from those that suffice for direct instruction. Classrooms designed as forums for discussion are more appropriate than lecture rooms. Adjacent rooms with private study bays are also necessary if pupils are to have the conditions they need for independent study.[9]

Children need some choice in the matter of private study. As long as all 'free' time is supervised we shall not know whether or not we have succeeded in motivating our pupils. If they are given a genuine choice between studying and 'wasting time' they will have new opportunities to mature. At the same time senior pupils will have an opportunity of relaxing during an often arduous school day. The sixth-former who prefers to read a novel or simply relax with his classmates instead of studying during a 'free' period will be able to do so. The kind of self-control we expect of senior pupils, and often fail to find, might well be developed in young people if we allowed them more freedom of action earlier in their school careers, even to the extent of providing more totally free time during the school day. Experiments in some European countries have demonstrated the advantages of reducing the amount of time spent on classroom studies. Where time for social and physical activities has been increased, gains have been noted not only in physical fitness but also in classroom achievement. In New Zealand, however, any increase in time spent outside the classroom would have to be accompanied by the provision of new facilities in our schools for both private study and a range of recreational activities.[10]

Class Groupings

Age and ability grouping is almost universally accepted in New Zealand secondary schools as the most efficient method of organising children for classwork. This system of grouping has been questioned in some countries on the grounds that it inhibits growth and develops undesirable attitudes and values. Where experiments have been conducted with other forms of class grouping, it has been shown that both the attitudes and performance of children are likely to be superior to those in streamed classes. It has been suggested that where children are streamed their performance is pre-judged and they become conditioned by their teachers' expectations.[11] Because of this the true abilities of some children are masked. There is evidence too that conditioning is restricted to the kinds of ability the teacher is expecting the children to develop; growth may occur outside the limits of his expectations but remain unrecognised by him. For example, a teacher may expect and find that a 'low-ability' stream is poor at memorising information but, when the class is tested for higher skills beyond his expectations, such as the ability to formulate hypotheses, significant growth may have occurred in spite of limited teaching.[12] Where classes are unstreamed, teachers learn to look for and encourage diverse growth in all children.

Streaming is meant to divide children into so-called 'ability groups'. But the measures used are unreliable and take little account of children's differing rates of development.[13] Furthermore, despite this unreliability, small changes in pupils' class position are used to promote and demote them from one group to another, a procedure which often causes them unnecessary anxieties and attributes an undeserved accuracy to teacher-devised tests.

Our over-confidence in our ability to grade children is nowhere better illustrated than in the selection and treatment of 'slow learners'. Because insufficient research has been done in this field our approach to these pupils remains largely intuitive, yet many schools quite confidently label certain pupils 'slow learners' on the basis of tests which measure a narrow range of abilities. What research has been done suggests that intelligence can be easily masked by environmental influences and that our best measures of intellectual potential are often unreliable.[14] And, where children of low initial attainment are placed in classes of mixed ability, there is some evidence that their growth is greater than when they are segregated for special treatment.[15]

Criteria for Judging Class Groupings

While surveying the research on class groupings the committee adopted the following criteria which were closely related to the educational aims accepted by its members:

Does the grouping:
1. give rise to mutual respect between children and promote their self-respect?
2. give maximum opportunities for pupil contribution?
3. lead to optimum intellectual attainment?
4. promote the ability to learn how to learn?
5. encourage teachers to expect diverse growth?
6. help teachers to become sensitive to the readiness for learning of individual pupils?

Experiments with various types of class grouping could be judged by these criteria and the findings used to clarify the issues involved for New Zealand teachers.

Unstreamed Classes

Experiments overseas, particularly in Sweden, have investigated the attainment of secondary pupils in unstreamed classes. The Swedish experiment found that several thousand Stockholm pupils who were grouped in heterogeneous classes (with abilities ranging from the highest down to an I.Q. of 70) performed as well in national examinations as an equal number of children of the same range of ability placed in streamed classes.[16] It should be noted, however, that no class in Sweden can be over thirty and, in fact, in 1966 the average size was twenty-two. The teaching load is also much smaller than in New Zealand. Nonetheless, these Swedish findings suggest that a similar experiment would be worth while in this country. It is significant that before the findings of the experiment were published 73 per cent of Swedish teachers preferred classes to be streamed and believed that attainment would be lower in mixed-ability classes.

In unstreamed classes pupils of relatively low initial attainment at first tend to benefit most; but those of high initial attainment quickly learn to increase and clarify their own understanding by helping others. For these latter children there is also the challenge of 'learning how to learn' when the teacher's energies are taken up with the less successful pupils. Moreover, advantages cannot be judged only in terms of classroom learning. Opportunities for social growth and for co-operative activity are likely to be greater in classes which are mixed in several variables, such as ability, socio-economic background and ethnic origin. In unstreamed classes also teachers tend to organise the learning so that each child is challenged according to his readiness. Teachers are thus encouraged to expect and cope with diverse growth. In a rigidly streamed class, where teachers are likely to be seeking a standard outcome, pupils whose rate of growth varies from the norm have little chance of special attention.

Stages of Attainment

In many secondary schools in the United States and in our own universities students are grouped in classes according to their level of attainment. Credit must be gained at each level of a subject before a student can proceed. Such a system will almost certainly develop in New Zealand between the fifth and sixth forms under the new single-pass School Certificate examination. This method of organisation is designed to ensure that in each class group the children begin at approximately the same level of attainment and readiness. Remedial work under this type of organisation could be regarded as a preliminary course of studies.

In the first year of secondary schooling tests would be used to place every child at a level appropriate to his previous experience and attainment. It would be essential to develop reliable ways of measuring attainment in all areas of learning. Unfortunately our present test measurements are quite primitive and give teachers little guidance in placing children.[17]

Class Groupings and the Curriculum

The method of grouping children depends to some extent on the way the curriculum is organised. Many schools in New Zealand have accepted a course structure which arranges children according to vocational needs; others have organised their classes so as to make team teaching possible. No doubt many different forms of grouping can be used to attain the same set of educational objectives—no inflexible plan is possible; but our knowledge of the processes of learning and group dynamics may help us to suggest appropriate models. In Section 4 'Learning and Enquiry' the committee has suggested such a model based on modes of enquiry, and in Section 6, 'The Curriculum' it has set out its thinking on tutor-seminars which could help children to learn to relate the parts of their educational experience.

School Councils

Outside the classroom there is also need for increased pupil participation. If young people emerging into adulthood are given no share in the organisation of the school community, their development of a sense of personal responsibility for their own behaviour and for that of others is retarded. Whether children recognise this or not, they rightly resent being directed by forces over which they have no control.

Pupil participation in school affairs can be attained through various forms of pupil government. The success of such experiments can be measured in terms of the extent to which the individual pupil believes his own views can be heard and the extent to which he feels he is significant in the school. If there is any pretence on the part of the staff or principal, children will quickly reject the experiment.

It is unfortunate that the nineteenth-century tradition which saw the pupil-teacher relationship as one of mutual hostility is still accepted in some schools. Learning sometimes occurs despite hostility—but through the inducement of external rewards rather than through the work of the teacher. In authoritarian conditions many young people inevitably develop resistance to learning. Alternatively, where pupils have a genuine part to play in school affairs, it is possible to establish a rapport between staff and pupils which encourages pupils to recognise that they are responsible to some degree for their own progress. Such rapport helps to establish learning situations which more readily lead to the development of desirable ends.

A system by which a range of school matters is discussed at form level and then brought before a student council by pupil representatives has proved acceptable in a number of New Zealand secondary schools.[18] Where the principal or staff are represented it is generally recognised that they are present as contributors and not as authorities. It has been found that council decisions, carried back to forms by representatives, are very much more readily accepted than those made directly by authority (for example by instruction at an assembly). The setting up of such councils in our schools gives children increased opportunities to practise democratic procedures, not only through elections but also at committee level where they can begin to develop respect for differing points of view. It has been noted that where prefects have become involved with council activities they tend to drop their 'police' roles and begin to see children not as subjects to be ruled but as young people in need of guidance. By becoming helpful advisers to younger children they no longer meet with resentment. The more that authority is vested in a prefect system alone, the more the stature and rights of younger pupils are reduced and the less responsibility and co-operation can be expected from them. Whereas prefects are answerable only to the principal and staff, members of a school council are accountable to the pupils themselves. This ensures that council members see their position not as a privilege or right but as a duty and responsibility.

Effective democratic procedures in a school provide opportunities for the voicing of pupil opinion and needs and give the school administration a way of communicating with children which can lead them to better understand the administrative needs of the school.

The committee feels that where opportunities do exist for pupils to participate in school affairs the incidence of irresponsible behaviour is likely to be reduced. Law enforcement is less often necessary where a community begins to develop its own sense of identity. When a school believes in its pupils' right to participate in their own organisation, maximum emphasis is placed on involvement for solving individual and community problems and minimum emphasis on penalties.

It is also clear that the development of effective school councils depends on commitment to the principle of prompt revision of their functions in the light of experience.

The Needs of Adolescents

The greatest impediment to the responsible growth of children is the tendency, at all levels of our school system, to bend children to conformity. Many adults feel that young people must conform to established social norms if they are to adjust successfully to life in the community. Yet, in a rapidly changing society, flexibility of mind and a capacity to make independent value judgements are the qualities most necessary if young people are to find security in change; such an emphasis is not inconsistent with the development in them of loyalty to a set of values, but these values should arise out of their own enquiries into human behaviour.[19] Young people drilled to conform to a static society may find it difficult to come to terms with the realities of the modern world. Some schools argue that conformity is needed to maintain standards and make efficient administration possible. Such arguments are appropriate only if we agree that human growth is greatest in a highly regimented environment. The ends outlined in this report cannot be achieved in this kind of environment.

Adults must try to understand the ways in which young people are growing and acknowledge that today's environment is very different from the one which shaped their own behaviour. Teachers can show this understanding by becoming sensitive to adolescent aspirations and by learning to accept young people for what they are and what they can become.

SUMMARY OF SECTIONS [1] AND [3]

Human Values and School Practice

A BASIS FOR JUDGEMENT

The committee places the highest value on:
1. the urge to enquire;
2. concern for others;
3. the desire for self-respect.

Mature Behaviour

Behaviour consistent with the qualities listed above includes the ability to:
1. accept the intrinsic worth and dignity of all human beings;
2. promote respect for others;
3. develop self-respect;
4. accept the right of others to their opinions and decisions;
5. attain self-knowledge and become aware of the effects of personal behaviour;
6. control emotional responses when the self-respect of oneself or others is likely to be diminished by its expression;
7. express one's feelings honestly;
8. grow to a sense of social responsibility;
9. develop a capacity for satisfying human relationships;
10. form consistent personal criteria with which to make independent judgements.

SCHOOL PRACTICES AND MATURITY

General

1. Present practices should be examined in terms of the attitudes and values they promote.

2. Schools should create opportunities for mature growth in all phases of school work.
3. Mature behaviour cannot be imposed from outside; it must be allowed to develop and to become valued through practice.
4. Schools have a responsibility to choose practices which promote desirable social ends as well as intellectual growth.

Motivation

1. Only when children's actions are increasingly determined by their own judgement and understanding will they grow toward maturity.
2. Motivation which arises from children's curiosity and is reinforced by their interest and involvement in what they are doing, will help them to learn how to learn.
3. In order to allow children the freedom necessary to develop their own motivation, teachers must be prepared to do things *with* children rather than *to* them or *for* them.

Competition

1. Competition often forces individuals and groups to behave in a manner inconsistent with principles of mutual respect.
2. Teachers who understand the effects of competition do not use it to motivate children.
3. If we find, through a thorough reappraisal of the effects of competitive practices, that they reinforce aggressive and thoughtless behaviour, we should be prepared to search for a rationale better fitted to our social needs.
4. In a non-competitive classroom, where individual contribution is valued, we can give opportunities for diverse growth instead of setting ourselves to turn out standard products.
5. Young people can grow by facing challenges which are relevant to their own interests and abilities; and by competing against their own standards, they can begin to participate in their own independent growth.

OPPORTUNITIES FOR RESPONSIBLE GROWTH

General

1. Children can grow in desirable ways even though their behaviour is not dictated by authority. Careful organisation and guidance

in the school and classroom can give rise to patterns of co-operative behaviour which are acceptable to young people and to their teachers.
2. Children can see the signposts to acceptable behaviour in the working situations the teacher creates.

New Learning Resources

1. New learning resources are urgently needed to help teachers to build classroom environments in which pupil contribution is valued.
2. Determination to uncover the processes and fundamental concepts of studies has placed the 'content' of facts and drills in a new perspective. Facts emerge and become valued as part of an experience whose goal is understanding.

Classrooms and Private Study

1. Classrooms designed as forums for discussion are necessary, and so are adjacent rooms with private study bays for independent study.
2. If pupils are given a genuine choice between studying and 'wasting time' in free periods they will have new opportunities to mature.
3. The kind of self-control we expect of senior pupils, and often fail to find, might well be developed if we allowed them more freedom of action earlier in their school careers, even to the extent of providing more totally free time during the school day.

Class Groupings

1. Criteria for the evaluation of class groupings.
   Does the grouping:
   (a) encourage mutual respect between children and promote self-respect?
   (b) give maximum opportunities for pupil contribution to learning?
   (c) lead to optimum intellectual attainment?
   (d) develop the ability to learn how to learn?
   (e) encourage teachers to expect diverse growth?

(f) help teachers to become sensitive to the readiness for learning of individual pupils?
2. Where experiments have been conducted with forms of class grouping other than streaming, evidence suggests that children's attitudes and performance are likely to be superior to those of pupils in streamed classes.
3. Where children of low initial attainment are placed in classes of mixed ability, present evidence suggests that their growth is greater than that when they are segregated for special treatment.
4. Opportunities for social growth and for co-operative activity may be greater in classes which are mixed in several variables, such as ability, socio-economic background and ethnic origin.

School Councils

1. If young people emerging into adulthood are given no share in the organisation of the school community, the development of a sense of personal responsibility for their own behaviour and for that of others is retarded.
2. Where pupils have a genuine part to play in school affairs it is possible to establish a rapport between staff and pupils which encourages pupils to recognise that they are responsible to some degree for their own progress.
3. A system by which school matters are discussed at form level and then brought before a student council by pupil representatives has proved acceptable in a number of New Zealand secondary schools.

The Needs of Adolescents

1. In a rapidly changing society, flexibility of mind and a capacity to make independent value judgements are the qualities most necessary if young people are to find security in change.
2. Adults must try to understand the ways in which young people are growing, and acknowledge that today's environment is very different from the one which shaped their own behaviour.
3. Teachers should become sensitive to adolescent aspirations and learn to accept young people for what they are and what they can become.

[4] Learning and Enquiry

Schools cannot succeed in promoting desirable social values until young people find their educational experience both challenging and relevant. Children who are not conscious of being involved in a satisfying search for knowledge and understanding will not readily feel the need for responsible action.

Knowledge, thought of as 'the sum of what is known', is a concept which is often used to include not only information, but also the consciousness of aesthetic, intuitive and physical experience. It is not the purpose of this report to attempt new definitions, but a deliberate distinction has been made between the factual aspects of knowledge and the thinking processes by which we make use of this knowledge. In much of the committee's work, members have distinguished between the ability of children to recall facts and principles and their ability to use them in new situations.

Benjamin S. Bloom, in the *Taxonomy of Educational Objectives* (1956), distinguishes between knowledge objectives which 'emphasise most the psychological processes of remembering', and ability and skill objectives which 'emphasise the mental processes of organising and reorganising material to achieve a particular purpose'.[1] It is these latter processes which generate new knowledge. This distinction is accepted for the needs of this report. Objectives concerned with the development of aesthetic appreciation will be discussed later in this section (*see below* pp. 33–36).[2]

LEARNING AND EXPERIENCE

Learning appears most relevant when it stems from direct experience; it is such experience which gives rise to meaning. The most useful direct experiences occur when children can work with and ask questions about the materials of a course; when, instead of being told about the matter being studied they have an opportunity to consider phenomena or data directly and to invent or select their own ways of problem-solving. This implies an inductive approach to learning which encourages children to ask questions and arrive at generalisations. In some disciplines, such as science, direct experience of many phenomena can be readily provided in teaching programmes. In others, such as history, although experience of events can rarely be first-hand, substitutes for direct experience in the form of copies of original documents and accounts, reproductions of contemporary visual material, artifacts and reconstructions can help children to recreate events. In this way they can be helped to use their imaginations to turn vicarious experience into something which is of direct relevance to them.

However, experience as such is neither a kind of knowledge nor a kind of enquiry. We may know or know about experiences, but experience is not the knowledge of experience: knowledge arises only through reflection on experience. It is one thing to experience breathing but quite another to know about respiration. Experience does not consist of assertions; it is neither true nor false: it simply is. Because of this, learning should be concerned with ways of reflecting on experience which lead to the generation of new knowledge. Experience for its own sake can be 'busy work'. Only when children become skilful at interpreting experience as a result of asking questions about it, will they gain new understanding from their school work.

It is useful to distinguish between ordered experiences and common experiences.[3] The latter include all the experiences we have without conscious effort. Ordered experiences, however, are the result of investigation, a process of deliberately making observations for the express purpose of answering questions, solving problems or testing hypotheses, theories, conjectures and conclusions. A classroom in which phenomena and data are examined, grouped, talked about and used to arrive at tentative conclusions will help pupils of all abilities to make use of this ordered experience. Their need is an active talking classroom where they can exchange ideas and develop the skills of enquiry.

Discussion is a major stimulus to thinking and learning. It is not just one way among others by which the mind is liberated; it is the main way whereby our more human qualities are developed and the underlying value of tolerance becomes accepted. Admittedly communication without mutual respect can often increase prejudice, but discussion can be highly educative, and so can conversation, provided the interactions are genuine and spontaneous, with the pupils saying what they want to say about matters which interest them. Where class discussion is helping young people to grow, we expect them to be as eager to formulate questions as to answer them. The test of such a classroom situation may be measured in terms of the number of challenging questions the pupils ask for themselves.

Because our present examinations demand large quantities of memorised information, much of it consisting of unrelated 'pieces', teachers tend to teach for information, and the development of genuine classroom discussion is inhibited. Teachers confronted with lengthy prescriptions feel they cannot allow children the kind of active experience with ideas which helps them to see the relevance of their work, both to their own personal growth and to their life in society. To prevent this situation from arising, prescriptions should be limited, thus allowing time for the free exploration of ideas; and examinations should be developed that stress a full range of mental skills, of which the ability to remember would be only one.

Assumptions about the Human Mind

Those who value discussion as an important aid to learning must believe that the mind grows best in a community environment. There is good evidence to support this belief.[4] Educationists see the human mind as interactive rather than passive, growing by a process of interplay with other minds.

Today measurement of the capacity of the mind is seen as an extremely complex study.[5] At the very least, intelligence must be thought of as a plural quantity, with some measurable aspects and others which have not yet been identified. Standardised tests have been developed to measure many of the known aspects of intelligence.[6] The use of a range of these tests to obtain a profile of some of a child's abilities is preferable to the situation where one figure is sometimes accepted as a reliable index of ability.

Many teachers prefer to judge the intelligence of their pupils on their performance in class and their capacity to work towards set goals. But in this there is the danger that the teacher may not know the level of a child's initial attainment before using his own courses as a measure of ability. It has already been noted that children presented with unrealisable goals will have their true abilities masked by frustration, a sense of failure, and a consequent dislike of learning. As has already been stated (*see above* pp. 17–18), it is unfortunately true that limited goals will limit attainment. Children categorised falsely will tend to perform according to a label which is not related to their true ability. For all teachers the most useful method of assessing ability is to identify the constituent skills in their own discipline and to attempt to measure achievement in these. This can be achieved partly through well-constructed class tests and partly through the use of standardised attainment tests.[7]

The Development of Mental Skills and Abilities

Research by B. S. Bloom, by the Swiss psychologist, J. Piaget, the educationist, J. S. Bruner, and others has shown that all mental abilities can be developed in very nearly all children.[8] Children can be brought to analyse information, see relationships and form generalisations. It has been demonstrated that these abilities are present as soon as a small child begins to explore his environment. The ability to organise relationships, to interpret, and to evaluate information and ideas are higher skills but they are also embodied in learning processes from a very early age.[9] Teachers can build on these natural skills and allow pupils to enjoy using them for diverse enquiries. This does not mean that all children need to be able to show evidence of a capacity for abstract thought in words or symbols. Many pupils can show these skills in the way they organise their work in quite practical situations. For example, in craftwork children can readily demonstrate their ability to analyse a project into its elements, perceive form, and evaluate the balance and design of the work. They do not need to talk or write about these skills. Their work is evidence enough.

The ability to see new connections between disparate ideas is probably the ultimate aim in all learning. This creative power in human thought stimulates rapid growth. It is a capacity which depends on judgement of what is relevant and on the ability to invent and plan for unfamiliar circumstances. This very high skill contributes to the flexibility of mind needed in a changing society; yet all children are known to be capable of profound and unique communications of this kind. If we have tended to doubt this in the past it may be that we have not been prepared to listen carefully to what young people were saying.

The lesson from developments in educational psychology is that most teachers underestimate children's capacity to see relationships and consequently restrict their opportunities to do so. This is particularly true for the less successful pupils in our secondary schools.

Content Courses and Ability Courses

The degree to which young people can develop specific skills and attitudes is determined by the kind of educational experience we give them. There are several types of course available which offer children varying experiences.

Some *content* courses are primarily concerned with facts and principles that must be remembered and topics that will lead to later understanding. Other courses which have a content emphasis, nevertheless claim to stress the development of enquiry skills and an understanding of key concepts.

The question asked by a third type of course is: What do we want children to be able to do after learning that they were unable to do before? Teachers who accept a behaviour-type course want to obtain objective evidence of children's achievement. This necessitates a clear statement of children's abilities and an evaluation of them clear enough for others to follow.

The advantages of the behaviour position lie in the fact that words like *understanding* and *knowledge* must be defined in terms of abilities: What do children *do* when they understand?[10] What do they *do* when they know? Any statement of objectives must therefore be a statement about the performances expected of pupils.[11] When successful behaviours or performances are known, evaluation is possible and teachers can begin to see new ways of bringing about changes in their pupils' thinking and attitudes.[12]

ENQUIRY

One of the most useful ways of changing the behaviour of young people is through enquiry. Enquiry-centred courses are designed to develop the fullest range of mental abilities and attitudes, and through this development to enable children ultimately to direct and control their own learning. They thus contribute to a major aim in all schooling: that of learning how to learn.[13]

A teacher who wishes to use enquiry methods must design and maintain conditions in which pupil enquiry can take place. These conditions must include freedom from external pressures. Rewards offered by the teacher and the asking of leading questions prevent an atmosphere of challenging enquiry from developing. The creation of a class situation where the rewards for interested investigation are inherent in the work in hand is hindered by competition for outside credits. Competing children are searching for 'right' answers, whereas children committed to enquiry are prepared for and expect diverse findings which will need to be debated and tested. Competition demands absolutes, but enquiry is aware of the necessary tentativeness of human conclusions.[14]

The teacher can also help children to examine the enquiry process itself so that they can understand how knowledge comes into being, where theories come from, and how they can be appraised. Such enquiry changes pupils from consumers of knowledge to 'producer-consumers'. Thus they learn to be able to evaluate the theories and conclusions of others and also to make their own contributions.

The Teacher's Role

The growth of enquiry is helped by co-operation, discussion and the building up of group knowledge from the contributions of its members. If pupils are to develop their own thinking structure, the traditional role of the teacher needs to be changed. Instead of being primarily a communicator of information he must become an adroit guide to the enquiry process. His questioning should focus not only on the substance under discussion but also on the mental operations needed to answer his questions, such as the ability to analyse data. Only where the teacher is conscious of these mental operations in terms of specific behaviours can he devise appropriate questions and judge the responses to them.

Enquiry and investigation also imply that children must learn to ask questions, both during class discussions and when they are working with the materials of a course. They will have little chance of developing this ability if the teacher deprives them of initiative and sets a bad example by asking a series of prepared questions designed to obtain a set of standard answers. If teaching is conducted according to an inflexible plan, and if conditions such as the size of the class make a quasi-military discipline necessary, learning is stultified.

The class lecture is particularly ill-suited for presenting materials that cannot be understood without periods of reflection. Enquiry followed by discussion is more conducive to understanding. Lectures, however, can be useful devices for acquainting pupils with the aims and design of a course and for outlining the related roles of classwork, discussion, homework and tests.

The Textbook

A good textbook should provoke thinking and discussion by providing the raw materials for enquiry and it should help develop interest in the discipline by asking penetrating questions that lead pupils to ask their own. It should stimulate further reading and help to elucidate concepts and principles by setting up situations which can lead pupils towards understanding. These principles and concepts should, of course, remain unstated in the text since they will be developed and expressed by the pupils in a form and language peculiar to their own level of development. A textbook should also contain enrichment material that goes beyond secondary school studies. Such a book might include a structured set of learning sequences including study questions, data of various kinds including documents, suggestions for discussion, self-testing items, ideas for home projects, sources of audio-visual materials and other learning aids.

Materials and other Learning Aids

More and more modern textbooks, particularly in science, are integrated with work manuals, teachers' guides and achievement tests. It has already been noted that this trend is helping teachers to concentrate on their central task of guiding their pupils' explorations. But when teachers use 'concept-centred' guides a traditional fact-giving orthodoxy must not be replaced by an equally narrow concept-giving orthodoxy. Enquiry demands flexibility and varied outcomes; if a teacher is to work towards these ends he must not follow a textbook slavishly. He must appreciate the enquiry process himself and constantly invent teaching situations which will best stimulate enquiry among his pupils. At best the textbook or guide is a reference prop, not a directive for minute-by-minute activities.

Motivation for Enquiry

Classroom techniques alone, however skilled, are unlikely to be very effective in furthering the understanding of school work; the material presented must form a pattern that has real meaning for the pupils at all times. A classroom technique may hold a pupil's attention for a few minutes, but for abiding interest children must have questions for which they seek answers. Motivation which stems from this desire for answers is tapped largely by means of the organisation and structure of the material being learned. This structure will take into account the logic of the subject area and the way in which children learn. Pupils who can appreciate the overall shape of a discipline are more likely to be able to transfer the experience they have gained.[15]

Evaluation of Enquiry

It is important to test the objectives we claim to be teaching. If we say we are teaching for understanding and the skills of enquiry, but test only the ability to remember, we shall set up in our pupils' minds undesirable tensions which will be resolved largely by their 'learning things off'. The evidence is overwhelming that evaluation has an important effect on what pupils learn and the way they learn it (*see below* Section 5). If we teach for enquiry we must examine for enquiry. Evaluation should be thought of as part of the learning process and should help pupils to become increasingly skilful at self-evaluation.

Modes of Enquiry[16]

Enquiry can be classified in terms of the kinds of experience drawn upon and the way in which the truth of statements is tested. Two major divisions are apparent on the basis of these criteria. The first, which might be called the empirical mode of enquiry, draws on ordered experience which results from deliberate, planned investigation. The statements produced are tested against this prepared experience. Scientific and historical research are examples of this mode of enquiry. The second mode may be called simply 'non-empirical' or possibly 'reflective'. This mode of enquiry tests its answers against its own logic, self-consistency and other accepted criteria for judgement. Mathematics and the arts are disciplines which call for non-empirical enquiry.

Endeavour in the arts may be thought of as being tested by 'affective congruency'.[17] Though the starting point of an enquiry in the arts will usually be 'private' experience—an essentially individual experiencing of phenomena—the creative enquiry in itself yields its own evolving experience. The object or situation being evolved (whether a play, poem, painting or dance) is its own testing ground. The artist responds *affectively* to the situation he creates until he reaches the point at which he feels no compulsion to further action: the *congruent* situation.

To distinguish between disciplines which share the same mode of enquiry, empirical or non-empirical, two questions must be answered:

1. What kind of questions does the discipline ask?
2. What is the process of enquiry and what kind of statements are made?

Empirical Mode

History is enquiry into past events and the process may be simplified to probing the past by examining documents, traces of the past and monuments in the light of suggested hypotheses and models. This mode is very much like enquiry in science; the primary difference between the two may be thought of as lying in the kinds of data that are interpreted. Some people may think also that there is some difference between the kind of generalisations made by history and science.

Science proceeds by induction to tentative generalisations and thence by deduction to the testing of new hypotheses and consequently to the testing of the generalisation itself—whether it be a 'law', a 'model' or a 'theory'—through appeal to the results of designed experiments. This deliberate setting up of hypotheses and the testing of them against selected documents or experimental results will be called 'investigation' in this report. Enquiries in history and science are therefore (a) empirical and (b) investigative.

Non-empirical Disciplines

Mathematics is concerned with symbolic relationships and requires only scant information from the environment to get under way. The outcome, results, theorems and statements of mathematics are not tested by appeal to experience. Internal consistency with axioms, logical development, and elegance are the criteria of 'truth' used by mathematicians. The fact that mathematics has many practical applications is irrelevant to the discussion at this point.

Art is an endeavour which is both non-empirical and non-investigative in essence. Science, history and many other disciplines contribute to the work of artists, but the reflective processes which result in art are essentially different from investigative procedures. The artist can perhaps, as has been mentioned, be thought of as testing his product for 'affective congruence' (*see above* p. 33). Further, one may think of artists as drawing on 'private' experience and of their enquiries as concerning the interaction between this private experience and their work. Part of the affective congruency test is no doubt concerned with 'economy' and this criterion—Occam's razor or the criterion of simplicity or economy is valued in all human thought and endeavour.

Other Disciplines

History, science, mathematics and art have been chosen to illustrate four principal ways in which new knowledge and understanding can

be generated. Each, it is suggested, is autonomous in relation to one or more of the following questions:
1. What experience does it draw on?
2. What questions does it ask?
3. What answering procedures does it adopt?
4. How does it test the truth of its assertions?

It would appear that all disciplines in the school curriculum can be questioned in the same way.

Questions Asked by Philosophy

Philosophy does not employ the *investigative* method of science, but in seeking to answer a wide range of questions it is concerned with empirical and non-empirical modes of enquiry.[18]

Philosophy may involve a study of events that actually occur, but it is also concerned with ethical questions. The resulting enquiry is non-empirical and analytical and has much in common with mathematics as a mode of enquiry.

Many philosophical questions require reflection on the modes of attack and findings of other disciplines. Many of the questions that young people seek to answer fall into this category: questions which are related to their view of the society in which they live. Section 6, 'The Curriculum', will suggest some ways by which young people can be given opportunities to satisfy the need to discuss their own society and the values it espouses.

The Universe of Enquiry

The diagram on p. 36 illustrates a possible comprehensive view of the whole field of enquiry, a field which leads to the continuous generation of new knowledge.

Here, art and philosophy are seen as 'taking in' all other kinds of experience and, chiefly through reflection, communicating private formulations from art and public formulations from philosophy. 'Public' statements are deliberately exposed to test and refutation whereas 'private' communications are ultimately assessable only by the artist himself.

ART might be thought of as using:
- painting
- pottery
- sculpture

dance
and other disciplines

as modes by which artists solve problems of a personal nature.

PHILOSOPHY raises questions concerning existence and the development of individuals and society, questions relating to values, and questions concerning the nature of enquiry.

These two disciplines permeate all other modes of enquiry but they are also sources for transforming information into new levels of perception, insight and perspective. In a sense all human beings are artists and all are philosophers, or rather all 'artify' and all philosophize.

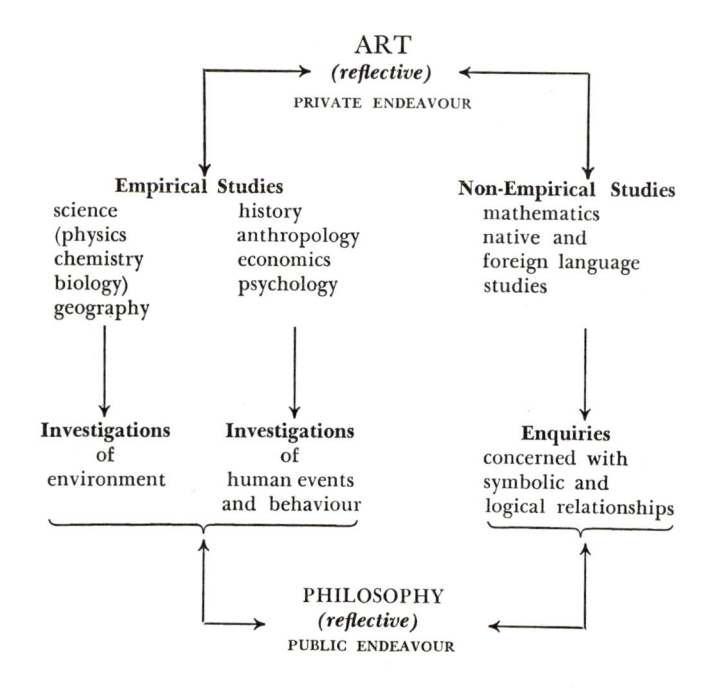

```
                          ART
              ┌────────► (reflective) ◄────────┐
              │       PRIVATE ENDEAVOUR         │
              │                                 │
              ▼                                 ▼
      Empirical Studies                Non-Empirical Studies
      science      history             mathematics
      (physics     anthropology        native and
      chemistry    economics           foreign language
      biology)     psychology          studies
      geography
         │             │                    │
         ▼             ▼                    ▼
   Investigations  Investigations        Enquiries
        of              of             concerned with
   environment     human events         symbolic and
                   and behaviour      logical relationships
   ╰──────────┬─────────╯              ╰────────┬────────╯
              │                                 │
              └────────►  PHILOSOPHY  ◄─────────┘
                         (reflective)
                       PUBLIC ENDEAVOUR
```

Enquiry and the Balanced Curriculum

The value of displaying the elements of various enquiries is that our attention is drawn to the significant ways in which we build our view of ourselves and of our environment. If enquiries of the kind discussed here lead to a wide range of new knowledge and insights, they may well suggest activities which should be included in a curriculum which seeks to promote the fullest growth in young people.

The curriculum should reflect a wide range of human endeavour and give children opportunities for participating in representative enquiries. A balanced course of studies would give children opportunities:
1. to reflect on a wide range of ordered and common experiences;
2. to raise questions about all aspects of knowledge and experience;
3. to develop skill in using the main human procedures for seeking answers—investigative, analytical, aesthetic and philosophic;
4. to understand the ways in which to test the truth of statements and conclusions.

A typical course of study representative of the main fields of enquiry should contain one or more disciplines from each of the following groups:
(The special significance of Group 5 will be discussed in Section 6, 'The Curriculum' (*see below* pp. 57–59)).

GROUP	MODE	PROCEDURE	DISCIPLINES
1	EMPIRICAL	Investigation of environment.	Science (physics, chemistry, biology), geography
2	EMPIRICAL	Investigation of human events and behaviour.	History, economics, anthropology, psychology.
3	NON-EMPIRICAL	Enquiries concerned with symbolic and logical relationships.	Mathematics, native and foreign language studies.
4	NON-EMPIRICAL	Aesthetic enquiries concerned with self-expression and communication.	Painting, pottery, sculpture, woodwork, music, technical drawing, clothing, literature, dance, cookery, physical education, drama, engineering.
5	EMPIRICAL and NON-EMPIRICAL	Analytical and reflective.	Philosophy, sociology.

NOTE 1

The disciplines have been grouped according to their dominant procedures. It should be remembered, however, that some disciplines do not fit entirely within the group in which they have been placed. Some include more than one procedure. When the engineer investigates materials he engages in science; when the musician looks at the development of music through the ages he engages in an historical investigation.

NOTE 2

Woodwork, engineering and technical drawing have been included for their educational value as vehicles for offering young people opportunities for satisfying aesthetic enquiries, not for their technological significance.

SUMMARY OF SECTION [4]

Cognitive Objectives

The following summary sets out the mental skills associated with the development of understanding and a capacity for problem-solving. These skills are stated as behaviours and are arranged approximately in order of increasing complexity.

THE ABILITY TO

memorise information.

interpret written and spoken statements and use relevant vocabulary when communicating.

analyse information and distinguish the relevant from the irrelevant.

predict by arguing cautiously beyond known information on the basis of trends observed within it.

apply principles in unfamiliar situations.

suggest generalisations after recognising trends in information.

suggest tentative hypotheses based on a knowledge of principles.

suggest ways of testing generalisations, explanations or hypotheses.

recognise accurate argument based on valid evidence.

organise relationships into a system by incorporating a network of generalisations into a theory, essay or report.

evaluate rival theories by testing them against known information and other criteria.

Although this list may not be exhaustive, it serves to illustrate some important behavioural outcomes of learning. The goals associated with the development of attitudes and values are listed in Section 5 (*see below* pp. 49–52). The committee is aware that skills associated with intellectual growth inevitably have an affective component, and that the development of attitudes and appreciations parallels the growth of mental skills. The separation of the two groups of behaviour into 'cognitive' and 'affective' is a convenience which helps to identify these aspects of human growth for the purposes of discussion and measurement.

Learning and Enquiry

The thesis of this section is the development in young people of the urge to enquire. The following statement summarises this thesis simply:

> *that*
>
> > *enquiry*
> >
> > > *promotes the ability*
> > >
> > > > *to learn how to learn —*

This ability subsumes all other competencies discussed in this report.

[5] The Measurement of Objectives

Learning is thought of in this report as a change in a person's ways of thinking, feeling and acting due to experience; in education experiences are organised to promote desired and specified changes, unlike life experiences, which are more random and less consciously controlled.[1] It follows from this view of learning that objectives must be formulated as clear statements of definite behaviours and that there should be ways of finding out whether the changes desired have been brought about. Teachers and curriculum specialists must then build learning experiences which will lead to these changes. The changes effected can be measured in terms of the proportion of pupils who have changed and/or the degree of change in individuals.*

It is important to distinguish between the kinds of changes mentioned above, and the more general aims and goals often stated in courses and syllabuses. For example, 'the development of good citizenship' is so broad and general an aim that it gives little guidance to the teacher who wishes to help his pupils to become good citizens. By contrast, an objective like 'the ability to relate principles of civil liberties and civil rights to current events' is more

---

* Although this section of the report is not concerned with the technical details of modern examining, the concepts of *validity* and *reliability* are essential to any discussion of educational measurement.

A test is *valid* when it measures what an examiner sets out to measure. For example, if an examiner claims to be measuring thinking skills and tests only for the recall of information, his examination is invalid in respect of its purpose.

The *reliability of a test* is based on the consistency of its measurements. Like a ruler, a test shold give comparable results when the same thing is measured several times. A test has high reliability if it gives similar results when set to different matched groups of children. Techniques for matching groups and for establishing test reliability are discussed by L. Nedelsky in *Science Teaching and Testing* (1955).

Marker reliability is established by comparing the scores awarded by different markers to the same set of scripts. When reliability is high, the marks given by the various examiners will be very nearly the same. Marker reliability is usually low on traditional essay-type tests and high on 'objective tests'. However, even when marker reliability is high, errors can still occur in the marking of individual scripts through, for example, lapses in the concentration of the marker.

40

specific and begins to give teachers and examiners some guidance to both the subject content and the mental skills which the students are expected to develop.

Initial statements of objectives should be made by teachers but the further clarification of their meaning should be the joint task of teachers and curriculum specialists.[2] A significant contribution in this field has been made by Benjamin S. Bloom and his co-workers. The *Taxonomy of Education Objectives* contains a useful classification of goals which can help teachers to state objectives in a form which is directly related to pupil growth. The cognitive objectives summarised at the end of Section 4 (*see above* pp. 38–39) were developed with the Bloom classification in mind.

The Limitations of Examinations and Tests

Before discussing the positive value of tests and examinations it will be useful to survey some of the present objections to examinations and to the quality of their measurements. The following list suggests some of the causes which have led many national examinations to defeat the aims of education. The comments are equally applicable to much internal examining and testing.

1. Pupils receive no personal information about their performance and therefore have no way of knowing the specific faults which they could correct.
2. Pupils do not see their papers and they rarely try to find out what a given mark means.
3. If the teacher does not teach the pupil again there is no hope of reteaching, but in any case reteaching is almost impossible if he receives no details of the pupil's performance.
4. Examinations tend to hold all pupils to a given set of tasks; they thus ignore differences in pupil growth and the need to give all children a sense of worth.
5. A 'fail' is often quite incomprehensible to a pupil who has worked hard on a given course.
6. Many examinations set no goals for future learning and the pupil puts the course behind him as quickly as possible.
7. Our present examinations rarely help to clarify the objectives of courses by placing candidates in situations which clearly require the application of a range of specific abilities.
8. Examiners' reports do not often help teachers to identify the examiner's objectives because these are not stated in terms of specific behaviours.

9. Many teachers centre their teaching around the limited kinds of learning required by the examinations; this tendency is reinforced if examination marks are used as a measure of a teacher's efficiency.[3]
10. Marking is often unreliable and even where reliability is established there are still errors. Because of this there is no case for differentiating between candidates on the basis of small differences in score.

A widespread recognition of these limitations has led many teachers to mistrust examinations and even weekly or daily tests. Some teachers have gone further and advocated the abolition of all testing. However rather than reject such powerful tools we should see how we can use them to work for education as conceived in this report.[4]

The Positive Values of Testing and Examining

The following list of some of the positive outcomes that can result from testing and examining has been drawn up after a survey of research in this field.[5]

Tests and examinations can:
1. provide pupils with information about their achievement;
2. reinforce desired learning processes;[6]
3. promote in pupils the ability and desire to make judgements about their own growth;
4. give a motivation for learning;
5. help pupils to learn how to learn;
6. give information about a pupil's readiness for future work;
7. provide data for research on pupil development;
8. allow for the diagnosis of strengths and weaknesses in individuals and groups;
9. act as a source of evidence and reassurance for teachers whose subjective impressions can be confirmed or corrected;
10. clarify objectives and give them operational meaning, i.e. the examinations indicate situations designed to test for specific objectives;*
11. help teachers to judge the worth of curricula and to review the total school programme;
12. help in the diagnosis of strengths and weaknesses in curricula.

---

* An objective becomes *operational* when teachers can understand clearly what it means in terms of abilities, and can follow and apply the procedures for measuring its achievement.

It is immediately evident that many, if not all, of these positive values can be achieved only where teachers and examiners are skilled in the design, marking and interpretation of tests, and where detailed information is made available to teachers in a form which they can relate to their pupils' needs. Teachers are unlikely to make appropriate modifications in the curriculum or in their organisation of instruction unless they know the examiners' aims and their pupils' achievement in relation to each specified aim. If the full diagnostic value of tests and examinations is to be exploited, teachers should have readily available information about the detailed marking procedures, the significance of the marks, part marks, item difficulties, item norms and test norms.

Testing for the More Complex Mental Abilities

It was for long assumed that understanding would automatically follow acquisition of the 'content' information of a course. The teacher's responsibility was to make sure pupils acquired the information and examinations were designed to appraise their store of knowledge. Belief in the automatic development of the more complex mental processes such as understanding is no longer very widely held.[7] If these abilities are aimed at they must be taught for and examined for. The higher objectives stated in the summary to Section 4, (*see above* pp. 38–39) are widely accepted as desirable ends for education, and it is hoped that future examiners' reports will discuss achievement in terms of these ends. Until examiners and teachers accept the need to promote them our schools and examiners will fail to develop learning much beyond the level of simple recall of information.

Tests designed to elicit higher mental skills avoid over-emphasis on isolated facts and stress instead ideas and concepts that have more general application. Questions involving *why? how? with what results? of what significance? explain, interpret* and *compare* (rather than *who? what? describe* and *name*) are more likely to produce responses that show evidence of mental growth. Facts and rules are important only to the extent that they are related to concepts and principles which the pupil can state in his own terms and apply to new situations. There is good evidence to suggest that the more complex mental skills which are important in the development of flexible minds are retained longer than the less complex ones. It is therefore useful to test for this retention after major units of work.[8] Examination of the ability to recall facts, terms and rules is more appropriate to occasional short tests, but even in these tests items which measure comprehension rather than recall lead to longer retention and the greater probability of transfer.[9]

Direct and Indirect Ways of Measuring Changes in Behaviour

When educational objectives are reduced to clear statements about desirable changes there are both direct and indirect methods of collecting evidence of their attainment. Direct methods follow from the statements themselves. For example, the objective 'skill in the interpretation of data' may be tested by giving the pupil new information and asking him to draw inferences from it. Such direct methods seem to be immediately valid with reference to the stated objectives. Free-response questions of this type provide opportunities for pupils to plan their communication, organise material and show initiative and divergent thinking. Unfortunately these questions take a long time to assess and require well-trained markers. However, structured free-response questions which permit original thinking can be marked to a very high degree of reliability between independent markers working from carefully defined criteria, and can be regarded as 'direct' tests of ability.[10] Their advantage lies in the high degree of validity it is possible to obtain with them.

'Objective' tests are indirect tests. For example, recall is tested by asking pupils to recognise; the ability to analyse data is tested by asking them to select from given alternatives. An advantage of such tests is that they can be marked easily and objectively, and results are therefore quickly available for summary and analysis. There is little doubt that 'objective' tests are capable of being designed to test mental ability at higher levels than those of recognition and recall.

There are, however, some aspects of 'objective' testing which need further investigation. Evidence suggests that when pupils' study habits become adjusted to such testing their scores become less valid as time goes on and bear less and less relation to the results of direct tests.[11] It is also suspected that 'objective' tests tend to favour the convergent thinker—the candidate who is quickly satisfied with a 'right' answer—and that the more imaginative and open-minded candidate has greater difficulty in eliminating alternatives. But one of the greatest problems with objective-type tests remains the high degree of skill required to ask good questions. Good objective tests can measure a wide range of objectives, but the skill and time needed to design them places them outside the competence of a busy teacher.

Both direct (free-response) and indirect ('objective') questions have a place in a comprehensive examination. It has already been noted that the examiner's task is to design questions which will measure achievement in the objectives of a course.[12] The preamble to the new School Certificate science syllabus makes an excellent statement of objectives and their relation to examination measurements.[13]

Motivation to Take Tests and Examinations

The motivations of our competitive world are not accepted by all pupils equally. Certainly many young people wish to get ahead through achievement and for them an achievement test may be a challenging, exciting experience. But cultural studies suggest that many other children—those with disturbed or poor home circumstances in particular—care little about social and educational values; for them the motivation to take examinations and tests may, under present conditions, be too weak for them to do themselves justice. Moreover, those who enjoy competitive examinations may be harmed because their desire to be highly placed may distort their behaviour and prevent responses which are 'typical' of them. An examiner who wishes to use his testing for predictive purposes must try to find out what a pupil *does do* rather than what he *can do*. The pupil whose prime motivation is to be better than others is more likely to show in his answer what he thinks the examiner wants rather than what he believes himself.

The motivation most helpful to valid testing is the candidate's desire that the score should give *him* a true index of his growth, his desire to find out the truth even if it is unpalatable. This is not the normal competitive desire, where a high score is sought whether it is meaningful or not. The situation in which the subject actually becomes a partner in testing himself is uncommon. Most often tests are autocratically conducted: something like 'Take this test and I shall decide what is to be done with you.' Most teachers would disclaim any intention of dictatorship, yet it is true that tests are usually for the private information of the teacher, who then bases recommendations on them.

Co-operation between tester and subject is not an impossible goal: it can be achieved by taking the subject into one's confidence as to the test's purpose and letting him feel that it gives him an opportunity to find out about himself. If the person taking the test or examination knows what characteristic it is measuring and why a fair measurement is to his advantage he will have little motive to give an untruthful picture of his opinions.[14] In this context testing is conceived as a means of finding out about the pupil in order to aid his growth. It follows that examinations should not be thought of as terminal but as part of a continuing educational process. Tests used for guidance are used *for* and *with* the pupil and not *on* him. In such tests it is important to minimise elements of competition and imposition from above: the pupil should take the test or examination because he wants to know the results. At the same time the tests must measure something of importance that is capable of detailed interpretation. Interpretation is likely to be adequate only if successive tests or examinations can be compared so that pupil growth in different behaviours can be noted.[15]

Examination motivation cannot be fully controlled, but a great deal can be done to make the results more valid than they are at present.

External Examinations in New Zealand

Our view of external examinations will depend on our view of the purposes of our schools. If we think of secondary schools as places whose chief purpose is to give pupils an entrance certificate to an occupation we shall tend to accept the present examination structure. The main thesis of this report is, however, that this should not be our schools' main function but that they should be largely concerned with promoting the total growth of children so that they can contribute to society in many ways both during their time at school and later as adults. This view of education does not accept 'final' measurements: examinations and tests can only be thought of as instruments for aiding further growth. It has already been noted (*see above* pp. 41–42) that external examinations, as they are conceived at present, fail to help this growth. Well-constructed class tests set and administered by teachers can fulfil the aims of evaluation, provided the teachers are well trained in this field. If pupils are to have effective guidance for their future learning, our present external examinations should be replaced by tests administered by teachers for their pupils' benefit.

Where employers and higher educational institutions want a comparative measure of young people's achievement they can be given the results of standardised diagnostic tests and achievement tests, and the data which the school has gained from the results of its own testing programme. Standardised tests can be selected that measure abilities relevant to the needs of pupils in a particular community. Some countries have already developed such tests which can be easily administered by individual schools.[16] The results of the tests, expressed as a profile of abilities, are far more reliable and valid than those attained by any external examination system. This profile, supplemented by school reports on qualities not readily measured by examinations, would therefore be a much more valuable guide to a future employer than the present lists of marks. A certificate outlining this interim development of a pupil's abilities could well replace the present examination results and in time could gain the confidence of employers and of the university. However, before any change of this kind can become effective a professional unit would have to be established to design and validate such tests and train teachers in their administration and interpretation. A change of the kind described, costly as it would be, would make sure that the most powerful tool in education could at last be used to encourage learning and to measure pupil growth accurately.[17]

The Measurement of Values, Attitudes, Interests and Appreciations

Most educational programmes claim to move towards or even to reach goals in this area. This report places central emphasis on these goals. But we cannot know whether they have been reached unless we can first say clearly and exactly what they are and work out ways of measuring progress towards them.

The committee has placed particular emphasis on the development of mutual respect between individuals. But what do young people have to do to convince us that they value this quality? Passive behaviour might suggest such a valuing: for example, the self-effacing child who says little and does not disturb his classmates or his teachers may be judged a respecter of persons; on the other hand it may be that he is simply afraid of human relationships. Because of the problem of interpreting the meaning of silence, we need to look for positive evidence of deeply felt attitudes. Is the child who is constantly involved in 'good works' our ideal here: the child who always volunteers for charity collections or extra classroom duties; is seen to help an injured classmate along the corridor; always holds doors open for his teachers and classmates? Most of us can suggest possible ulterior motives for any or all of these actions. They may show that a child is a respecter of persons, but they may also prove to be automatic habits and not the result of thoughtful consideration.

Such behaviours can be counterfeits of respect; politeness sometimes falls into this category. Of course we must not discourage these actions simply because we are not sure of the motives for them, but we cannot accept them *per se* as clear evidence of respect.

It is probable that we can resolve this question only by looking for a pattern of behaviour which will reveal the motives behind action. Perhaps it is not the big actions that give us the best clues, but the small actions that often pass unnoticed in the school. The child who often makes a worth-while contribution to class discussion yet also listens carefully and courteously to what less gifted classmates say, is almost certainly giving us evidence of his attitude towards others. The quality of a child's listening is perhaps one of the most telling measures of his respect for other people. Again the child who refuses to 'show off' his superior skills in the presence of others whose self-respect could be diminished thereby, may be showing true respect: for example, a good gymnast who does not advertise the fact deliberately during routine physical education classes. Also a person who values the self-respect of others is probably not readily drawn into 'taking sides' in a discussion; he does not either attack intemperately or take umbrage unnecessarily—both behaviours calculated to reduce the self-respect of others. It seems that the key to mature action is the genuine wish to accept and encourage the individuality of others. Evidence of this wish is often neither dramatic nor obvious, but the trained observer who is sensitive to the implications of human actions can readily note signs and evaluate them.

It is often assumed that appropriate attitudes will develop, or certain lasting interests will be aroused, as a direct result of the development of mental abilities. Research seriously challenges this kind of assumption.[18] Evidence suggests that suitable kinds of learning situations are needed to promote the growth of specific interests and attitudes. These should include activities such as reading under the stimulus of study questions, role-playing and discussions about the feelings and reactions of individuals and groups in reported and real-life situations. It must be remembered, however, that 'thinking' and 'feeling' objectives overlap considerably and the distinction between them is artificial, though extremely useful when discussing educational aims.

Besides direct observation, the major testing procedures in the 'feeling' area of learning (interests, attitudes, appreciations and values), are by means of questionnaires, inventories, essays and structured essays, structural situations and interviews, unfinished stories and role-playing.[19]

Before such instruments can be satisfactorily designed it is again essential to state the behaviours being measured in operational terms. D. R. Krathwohl and his collaborators have made an important contribution towards this end. They have classified the 'feeling' objectives (called affective aims) and have made statements about specific behaviours which clarify the meaning of the objectives. In addition they have displayed test models to help examiners to test achievements in these areas.[20]

Objectives here are thought of as being associated with the development of 'a feeling tone, an emotion, or a degree of acceptance or rejection'. On Krathwohl's scale these objectives range from a primitive kind of 'awareness' through 'responding', 'valuing', 'organisation' and 'characterisation of a value or a value complex'. This last comprises statements about the mature whole person.[21] Each of the main categories is broken down into subdivisions and the meanings of each are clarified. Some of the higher categories, expressed in terms of attitudes such as 'open-mindedness' and 'intellectual honesty', are included in the objectives of a number of revised New Zealand syllabuses, for example, the new Science syllabus for School Certificate. In the area of human values the major objectives stated in this report can all be seen to have a place on the Krathwohl scale.

The following list of objectives is not meant to be exhaustive. It illustrates some of those in the affective area which have been named in this report. Not all of these statements are sufficiently operational to be of direct use to teachers. It is still necessary to specify a set of detailed behaviours for each objective so that a teacher can determine whether or not the objective is being attained. For example, under the heading '*VALUING*' a stated objective is that a pupil should value mutual respect. Earlier in this report (*see above* pp. 47–48) an attempt was made to delineate the behaviours which might be associated with the achievement of this goal. The individual teacher must attempt the same exercise for all the objectives he accepts in this area. If he is to make judgements about the attainment of goals he must have a basis for them.

CATEGORY	EDUCATIONAL OBJECTIVES WHICH ILLUSTRATE GOALS IN THE AREA OF VALUES, ATTITUDES, INTERESTS AND APPRECIATIONS
1.0 *RECEIVING* (*Attending*)	
1.1 *Awareness*	Develops a consciousness of colour, form, arrangement and design in the objects and structures around him and in the descriptive or symbolic representations of people, things and situations.

Recognises that there may be more than one acceptable point of view.

Becomes aware of the feelings of others whose activities are dissimilar to his own.

1.2 *Willingness to receive*

Attends carefully when others speak — in direct conversation and in groups.

Listens to others with an appearance of respect.

Appreciates with tolerance the cultural patterns exhibited by individuals from other groups: religious, social, political, economic and racial.

Increases in sensitivity to human need and pressing social problems.

1.3 *Controlled or selected attention*

Becomes sensitive to the importance of keeping informed on current political and social matters.

Becomes alert to human values and judgements on life as they are expressed by others.

2.0 RESPONDING
2.1 *Acquiescence in responding*

Is willing to comply with restrictions on his own actions that are necessary for the growth of others.

Is willing to participate with others in group activities.

2.2 *Willingness to respond*

Responds with consistent active and deep interest to intellectual stimuli.

Contributes to group discussion by asking thought-provoking questions or supplying relevant information and ideas.

Accepts the desirability of exploration and tentative choice before making decisions.

2.3 *Satisfaction in response*

Takes pleasure in conversing with different kinds of people.

Enjoys participating in varied types of human relationships and in co-operative group undertakings.

3.0 *VALUING*
   3.1 *Acceptance of a value* — Values mutual respect.

        Feels himself a member of groups which undertake to solve common problems.

        Has a sense of responsibility for listening to and participating in public discussion.

   3.2 *Preference for a value* — Assumes responsibility for drawing reticent members of a group into conversation.

        Shows interest in enabling other persons to obtain satisfactions.

        Deliberately examines a variety of viewpoints on controversial issues with a view to forming opinions about them.

        Discriminates between the many ideas commended to him.

   3.3 *Commitment* — Is conscious of the intrinsic worth of all human beings.

        Promotes the self-respect of others.

        Has a sense of responsibility not only for his own actions but also for the actions of others.

        Respects the right of others to hold their own opinions and make their own decisions.

        Does not become aggressive when confronted with statements with which he disagrees.

4.0 *ORGANISATION*
   4.1 *Conceptualisation of a value* — Forms consistent personal criteria which will allow him to make independent judgements.

        Relates his own standards of behaviour and personal goals by discussing them with others.

   4.2 *Organisation of a value system* — Accepts an emotional adjustment to the limitations inherent in his own aptitudes, abilities and interests.

        Judges peoples of various races, cultures and occupations in terms of their behaviour as individuals.

			Learns to know himself so that he can see clearly the effects of his behaviour, and learns to control those actions which diminish his own or others' self-respect.

Is able to control emotional responses when appropriate.

5.0 *CHARACTERISATION OF A VALUE COMPLEX*

    5.1 Generalised set   Is ready to revise judgements and to change behaviour in the light of evidence.

Readily changes his mind when new facts or insights demonstrate the need for revision of opinions formerly held.

Promotes open-minded examination of present trends and prejudices.

Makes decisions consistent with full enquiry, but also learns to appreciate the value of withholding judgement where he has insufficient experience or knowledge.

    5.2 *Characterisation*   Knows himself and others for what they are and what they can become.

Has a deep concern for the welfare of others and a sense of responsibility for society.

Believes that humanity should be evolving towards a greater understanding of its own behaviour.

NOTE
The categories and some examples in the list above are Krathwohl's; the remaining examples have been selected from the text of this report.

If value and attitude objectives can be defined with appropriate precision, it may be no more difficult to produce changes in this area than it has been to produce them in the patterns of thought of young people (though neither is easy to attain). But the problems in this area are different and teachers, curriculum specialists and research workers will have to do much before it is as well understood as the field of mental growth. Some of the higher categories listed above may take young people many years to reach. No one will reach all of them. Such goals call for a high price of commitment and effort on the part of school staffs.

Even where a school is teaching for values, attitudes, interests and appreciations, a teacher will rarely teach pupils long enough to evaluate changes. There is a real need to build co-ordinated evaluation procedures which will allow for the measurement of these 'affective' objectives during the whole period of a pupil's schooling.

The Relationship Between Intellectual Development and the Development of Attitudes

It has already been noted (*see above* pp. 39 & 48) that the classification of objectives into those concerned with the development of mental skills and those associated with attitudes, values, interests and appreciations, is largely artificial. Krathwohl himself has discussed the relations between the two groups of objectives. For example, attending to a phenomenon is a prerequisite to knowing about it, and only where one is willing to attend will one be able to learn. Hence *RECEIVING* could include the abilities of comprehension, application and analysis which are usually listed as mental skills.

A large part of what we call 'good teaching' consists in the teacher's ability to promote interests and appreciations through challenging young people's fixed or implicit beliefs and getting them to discuss issues. Certain mental skills can be used as a prerequisite to achieving such ends. For example, a pupil who learns ways of analysing a literary statement may find that new appreciations of nuances of human behaviour open up to him. It is also true that the misuse of a critical and analytical approach to learning—one which leads, for example, to the fragmentation of a literary work—lessens appreciation. Krathwohl cites as an example the bad effects of an over-careful and too detailed study of 'good' English classics.

Though courses may begin with statements about interests and appreciations, there is often a tendency for these aims to be lost sight of. It is easier to teach for very limited memory-type objectives because they are easily tested. Interests, feelings and attitudes are more difficult to evaluate, and consequently many teachers neglect this area of learning. If teachers become more conscious of these affective objectives and of the instruments available for measuring them, they may learn to place greater emphasis on them.

An approach to mental achievement through the development of interests, attitudes and motivations is of growing importance. The positive aspects of motivation, for example, self-discovery as a means of fostering interest and enhancing curiosity, may be building on a basic drive: a need for competency and for a feeling of effectiveness.

If we can develop in every child interest in what he is learning, and an appropriate set of attitudes and values about his intellectual pursuits, he may attain intellectual skills more rapidly.

An important difficulty in measuring interests and attitudes is that the behaviour we wish to know about is not what the pupil *can do* but what he *does do*. Pupils who are asked to display their attitudes or interests are often placed in an artificial situation and may not give responses that are typical of them. As previously noted (*see above* pp. 45–46) attitudes produced for test purposes must be treated with caution; if a pupil is trying to please or to get a good mark we are not likely to learn his true attitudes. Probably the best measurements are those made by direct observation when conditions are 'normal' and pupils unaware of evaluation. At the same time, if a pupil genuinely wants to know more about himself and is not concerned with 'success', inventories and questionnaires can be very useful.

SUMMARY OF SECTION [5]

Evaluation of Growth

Definition of Learning: A change in a person's ways of thinking, feeling and acting due to experience.

Measurement

Change can be measured in terms of the proportion of pupils who have changed and/or the degree of change in an individual.

Examinations

Examinations have significant effects upon the teaching and learning that actually take place in our schools, and, rather than reject such powerful tools, we should see how we can use them for the benefit of young people.

The Positive Values of Testing and Examining

Tests and examinations may:
1. provide pupils with information about their achievement;
2. reinforce desired learning processes;

3. promote in pupils the ability and desire to make judgements about their own growth;
4. give a motivation for learning;
5. help pupils to learn how to learn;
6. give information about a pupil's readiness for future work;
7. provide data for research into pupil development;
8. allow for the diagnosis of strengths and weaknesses in individuals and groups;
9. act as a source of evidence and reassurance for teachers whose subjective impressions can be confirmed or corrected;
10. clarify objectives and give them operational meaning, i.e. indicate situations designed to test for specific objectives;
11. help teachers to judge the worth of curricula and to review the total school programme;
12. help in the diagnosis of strengths and weaknesses in the curriculum.

Testing for the More Complex Mental Abilities

If the achievement of the more complex mental processes is aimed at they must be taught for and examined for.

Direct and Indirect Tests

Both direct (free-response) and indirect ('objective') questions have a place in a comprehensive examination. Indirect questions are valuable for testing recall, recognition and the less complex mental abilities, and direct questions for measuring the growth of more complex skills.

Motivation

1. The motivation most helpful to valid testing is the candidate's wish that the score should give him a true index of his growth.
2. Examinations should not be thought of as terminal but as part of a continuing educational process. Tests used for guidance are used *for* and *with* the pupil and not *on* him.

External Examinations in New Zealand

1. To give pupils effective guidance for their future learning, our present external examinations should be replaced by tests administered by teachers for the benefit of pupils.
2. If employers and higher educational institutions desire a comparative measure of young people's achievement at school, the results of standardised diagnostic and achievement tests should be made available to them.
3. These results, expressed as a profile of abilities, would be far more reliable and valid than the results of our present external examinations. This profile, supplemented by school reports on qualities not readily measured by standardised tests, would be a much more valuable guide to a future employer than a list of marks.

Measurement of Attitudes

1. It is often assumed that appropriate attitudes will develop and certain lasting interests will be aroused as a direct result of the development of mental abilities. This assumption is seriously challenged by research. Evidence suggests that suitable kinds of learning situations are needed to promote the growth of specific interests and attitudes.
2. If value and attitude objectives can be defined with appropriate precision, it may be no more difficult to produce changes in this area than it has been to produce changes in the patterns of thought of young people (though neither is *easy* to attain).
3. Some of the higher affective goals may take young people many years to reach. No one will reach all goals. Such goals call for a high price of commitment and effort on the part of school staffs.
4. An important factor in the measurement of attitudes is that the behaviour we wish to know about is not what the pupil *can do* but what he *does do*. Probably the most useful measurements can be made by direct observation when conditions are 'normal' and pupils unaware of evaluation.

[6] The Curriculum

The selection and organisation of a balanced curriculum must depend on two major considerations:
1. The educational aims of the school or school system.
2. An understanding of the learning process.

EDUCATIONAL AIMS

The educational aims of the committee may be conveniently summarised as:
1. to help young people to acquire values which will aid their individual growth and social consciousness;
2. to develop a capacity to enquire in representative fields of study.

To these we must now add a third major aim:
3. to develop in young people an ability to relate the parts of their educational experience so that they can see this experience as relevant to their lives.

The committee has been led to include this third major aim by the realisation that children today often leave our schools without any clear idea of the point or purpose of much of their school experience. Traditionally we have taught in specialised compartments without making any attempt to allow children to see the value of their whole schooling in perspective. If this attempt is not made we shall continue to deprive children of the capacity to measure the relevance of their school work.

Relating Experience

There seems to be only one way to help children to use the values and enquiries developed at school: *they must be given frequent opportunities to apply their total school experience to solving problems and answering questions that are of vital importance in their own lives.* Any attempt which asks them to use this experience to solve problems that *may* occur in their later lives seems to ignore the fact that they are *already living* throughout their school careers and have innumerable formed and partly-formed questions to which they wish to find answers as soon as possible. If young people are not given opportunities to discuss these questions within the school they will tend to face their problems introspectively, without guidance, without the 'fresh air' of open discussion, and without the reassurance that they are not alone in their preoccupation with these questions.[1]

They not only need opportunities to discuss questions, but also help in formulating their questions in a way that will help them to search for answers. To those who argue that adolescents lack the capacity to tackle the major questions of life, one can only answer that, if this is so, the lack has been contrived in part by the education system itself, and the sooner we can liberate the minds of our young people the sooner we shall be able to take advantage of the profound contributions they can make to our society.

Several kinds of organisation can be used to help children to relate the parts of their school work.

1. A single teacher may take them for all their school studies.
2. Teacher teams may work closely together with groups of classes.
3. Class tutors may be appointed with the sole task of taking certain classes at regular intervals during the school week and using these occasions to help children see the relevance of all their work.
4. Class teachers or class tutors may work in close consultation with other teachers or teacher teams.

Whatever the organisation, the purpose would be to give children opportunities to bring all their skills and experiences to bear on major problems arising out of their own concerns.

All four approaches could be included in one school organisation. Already in some schools certain groups of children are timetabled with one teacher for the greater part of the week. In others team-teaching is highly developed, although not for the purpose discussed here; and in most schools the form teacher fulfils in part the function of a tutor. However, present practices do little to help children to see their education whole and to see it alive.

The Functions of a Class Tutor

To achieve the end of relating knowledge more time must be given and a new kind of teacher must be trained. One of our present trained specialists is unlikely to be capable of acting as focus for children's discussion over the whole range of their experience. A tutor-teacher would not need to be a specialist in all fields of study, but he would need to understand the principal methods of enquiry. His function would not be to provide children with answers but to help them to enquire with all their cognitive skills and to direct them to reference material when it was needed. In short, he would need to be both an able chairman and a researcher of background material.

As an example, a question which most children are certain to ask during their school lives, is:

'*Why do racial tensions exist and how can they be resolved?*'

A question of this magnitude and immediacy, although part of the work of a good social studies course, requires all modes of enquiry to be brought to bear on it. Approaches developed in history, geography, economics, literature, language and art are relevant, but so too are those of the sciences and mathematics. Thus aspects of the problem might well be studied in terms of scientific (empirical—investigative) modes: the terms of the problem carefully defined, models set up, hypotheses formed, ways of gathering data designed and the outcomes reported as probability or statistical statements.[2] Scientific journals contain many accounts of such investigations into social phenomena. In this way pupils could be helped to use investigative skills developed in a wide range of disciplines and could then go on to examine in a rational and fruitful fashion points of view expressed in history, literature, art and the mass media.

Debate on a question of this kind would offer a flexible approach to many elements of the curriculum and would be a response to pupils' need to seek an answer to a particular question.

Teachers as an Educational Team

At present, with schools staffed by specialists, the first necessity for relating knowledge would be a total team approach. That is, teachers should be required to work together so that they begin to understand and appreciate the contribution each is making to children's education. This could not be done unless the school was conscious of its aims and all staff members were committed to their attainment. A teacher need not become proficient in all disciplines in order to understand the contribution they make and the nature of enquiry in them. A teacher of history *can* understand the approaches of science and a science specialist those of history teaching and the learning processes in that field.

Teachers who are sensitive to the totality of their own experience will the more readily see the need to understand the purposes and approaches in all aspects of the school's work. The teachers' colleges must play an important part in helping our teachers to approach this whole view of education.

Curriculum criteria that emerge from an understanding of the learning process

We must ask of the curriculum a number of questions which stem from our understanding of the learning process. These questions arise when we explore the effectiveness of the curriculum's contributions to the realisation of educational aims. An effective curriculum must take into account the needs of society, the psychological needs of children, the organisation of learning experiences and, finally, the opportunities for learning provided by the school system.* The following questions asked of the whole curriculum are equally applicable to separate disciplines.

PSYCHOLOGICAL NEEDS

Will the curriculum help to resolve unsatisfactory tensions in young people and facilitate their adjustment to the school community and to society?

This question may be broken down into further queries which help us to determine the kinds of tension that should be resolved and the conditions necessary for adjustment:

1. is co-operative behaviour consciously promoted?
2. are children helped to achieve a sense of identity and of belonging in the school community?
3. is their self-respect assured at all times?
4. is their curiosity fostered?
5. is there adequate provision for the success and sense of achievement of all children according to their abilities?
6. are there opportunities for them to ask and actively to seek answers to pressing questions?
7. are there opportunities for them to meet challenges which will ensure their optimum growth?[3]

All these questions are closely associated with the aims set out in this report. They must be asked not only in general of the whole school system but also in particular of the curriculum. This report contends that aims are desirable in so far as they are consistent with the psychological needs of young people. If we satisfy these needs we shall be well on the way to providing an environment in which relevant learning can take place. *The curriculum should therefore be thought of as a vehicle for the attainment of goals and not as an end in itself.*[4]

---

* The needs of society have been discussed in Sections 2 and 3 above.

ORGANISATION FOR LEARNING

The following sequence summarises the teacher's main tasks when organising for effective learning. He must determine his pupils' readiness for classwork, make sure his programmes have structure and relevant problem-solving opportunities and finally see to it that he can evaluate pupil growth adequately.
    Readiness
    Structure
    Problem-Solving
    Relevance
    Evaluation

Readiness

Is the curriculum sensitive to the readiness for learning of children of differing abilities?

The study of readiness is much more than an attempt to forecast success and failure; it is an attempt to match educational experiences to a child's characteristics. Readiness is affected by all his characteristics: his biological growth, his ideas and skills, his habits, his experiences in life, and his attitudes and values. A curriculum which is conscious of the need to determine readiness before allowing children to embark on a course of study must have built into it valid and reliable ways of assessing their characteristics. (In Section 5 above, some methods of assessment have been explored.) A school that ignores this need will unwittingly arouse resistance to learning by facing pupils with inappropriate class work. Sensitivity to readiness, however, will not in itself help teachers to devise worth-while learning situations; programmes are needed which have been designed specifically for children of differing ages, abilities and social backgrounds.[5]

The Structure of Disciplines

1. *Does each discipline include the basic concepts which give it order and meaning?*
2. *Can the content materials be organised so that effective learning is possible?*
3. *Does each succeeding period of study build on the ideas, skills, values, interests and attitudes of previous learning?*

Every discipline can be defined in terms of its structure.[6] This may be thought of loosely as the 'shape' of the study, but certain specific elements of this 'shape' should be noted. The central element is the mode of enquiry appropriate to the discipline. But the structure of a discipline also depends on its procedures, the object of the study, its language, its hierarchy of concepts, the persistent themes within it and its way of verifying its 'truths'. The structure of mathematics depends, for example, not only on its non-empirical mode of enquiry, but also on its analytical procedures, its preoccupation with relationships, its symbolism, its chain of deductive generalisations and its concern to invent new abstract generalisations which arise out of its own logic and are verified by it. Its ways of operating, its purposes, its language, its themes and verifications are not duplicated in any other field of study. If a study can be seen to have these elements of structure, it can be readily organised for learning. It has within itself a logical development and purpose which can be communicated to young people. But, if a field of study lacks these unifying elements, it appears as a set of discontinuous units of work which do not make sense as a whole.[7]

Once the structural elements of a discipline have been identified it is possible to break it down into progressive stages for learning. The least sophisticated language, concepts and themes will be studied early and the more complex ones later when the pupils are ready for them. The mode of enquiry and the procedures will be constant throughout the study and become more and more useful as the course proceeds.

Problem Solving:

Will pupils learn
1. *to understand and to ask the kinds of questions appropriate to each area of study?*
2. *to use the procedures needed to find answers to these questions?*

Certain types of questions are appropriate to particular disciplines. Children should know this and be able to use a discipline's procedures in order to find an answer. For example, the question, 'Why do men go on strike?' should be recognised as one that can be answered by using the investigatory methods of history and allied social sciences rather than those of other disciplines such as science. In order to reach a conclusion (even a tentative one) this would necessitate a wide survey of documents and opinions about the rise and present condition of the trade-union movement and some discussion of the psychology of groups. If children take part in this kind of enquiry they may become less likely to make prejudiced judgements.

Relevance

> *Is the curriculum relevant to the pupils' individual and social needs?*

The question of relevance has already been discussed at many points in this report.* It remains to make a distinction between individual and social relevance. Many experiences are intensely personal and appear to contribute to our growth without having any obvious social significance. The pupil who is engrossed in developing skills and insights in a particular art form is apparently not doing anything that contributes directly to his social role, and yet for his own growth the activity is particularly important. As long as his love of art does not conflict with mature relations with other people, we should accept it as an important component of self-enrichment. All young people must be given every opportunity to express their individuality in a creative fashion; indeed this expression will be an important influence in the personal development of many of them.

Evaluation

> 1. *Does the curriculum provide for adequate teacher evaluation of pupil growth?*
> 2. *Does it help children to evaluate their own progress?*

These questions have been discussed at length in Section 5 above. Learning is likely to be ineffective if the measurements of achievement are inadequate, for evaluation helps young people to understand the nature and quality of their growth.

OPPORTUNITIES FOR LEARNING

Opportunities for learning are a corporate responsibility. The following headings are therefore linked with questions which all people interested in the future of young people should ask, especially those who shape our educational policies. A curriculum which does

---

* See Sections 3 and 4 and the present section pp. 57-59.

not give young people opportunities to become engaged in the practice of enquiry, to value its lifelong importance, and to work with adequate resources cannot fulfil the educational aims discussed in this report.

    Practice
    Engagement
    Life-long Learning
    'Vocational' Education
    Resources

Practice

Does the curriculum give practice in representative modes of enquiry?

A balanced curriculum will develop in young people all the skills and attitudes they need to approach the solving of the problems they will face throughout their lives. Their real need is to understand how to formulate questions and how to set about finding useful and satisfying answers to them. As already noted, no one method of enquiry is sufficient for this purpose (*see above* pp. 33-38). A student who demands empirical proof of the truth of all human thought will ignore the wide range of insights that have been developed on premises that are not susceptible to the rigours of this kind of proof.[8] This report begins with such a premise: 'that it is desirable that man show a concern for the welfare of his fellows.' Recognition of the fact that much of our action stems from such an 'act of faith' is as important as realising that some phenomena can be investigated with logical precision. A balanced curriculum should therefore provide opportunities for young people to engage in all modes of enquiry, and to achieve this a flexible pattern of studies is necessary.

The diagram below illustrates a way of dividing the curriculum into four important fields of study each of which contributes to enquiries conducted under the guidance of a class tutor (or teacher team).

Painting, pottery, sculpture, woodwork, music, technical drawing, clothing, literature, dance, cookery, physical education, drama and engineering are all equally capable, if properly structured, of giving young people opportunities to solve problems of an aesthetic nature (*see above* Section 4, pp. 33-38). No strict proportion of these studies should be mandatory on schools or on children. The principal and staff of a school, aided by expert advice, will always remain the best judges of the extent to which these activities should be made available to children. But they must make sure that, whether they are taken singly or in any selected combination, they will achieve aesthetic ends. If criteria such as those set out in this section are accepted, all these modes of action are capable of helping children to attain satisfaction and enjoyment in self-expression and communication. None of these subjects should be regarded as any more or less significant than any other, and none should be seen as essential for the growth of *all* children.

CURRICULUM ORGANISATION

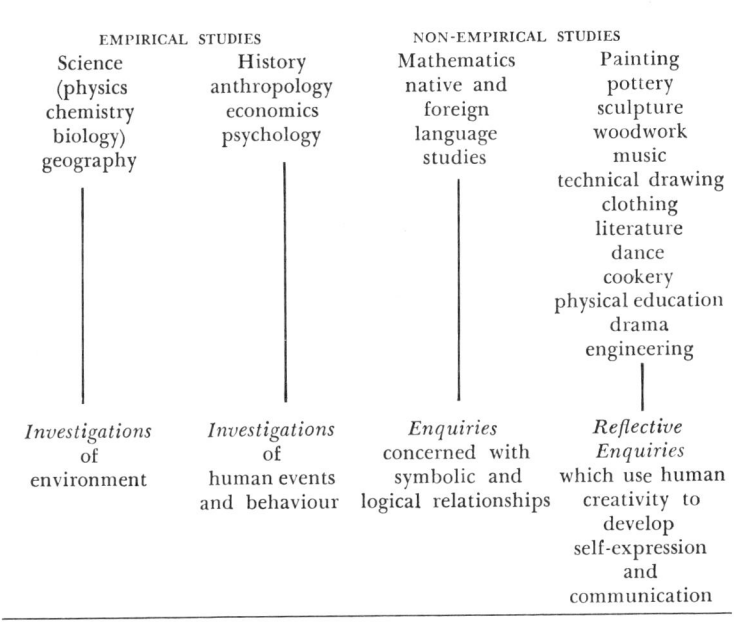

EMPIRICAL STUDIES		NON-EMPIRICAL STUDIES	
Science (physics chemistry biology) geography	History anthropology economics psychology	Mathematics native and foreign language studies	Painting pottery sculpture woodwork music technical drawing clothing literature dance cookery physical education drama engineering
Investigations of environment	*Investigations of human events and behaviour*	*Enquiries concerned with symbolic and logical relationships*	*Reflective Enquiries which use human creativity to develop self-expression and communication*

EMPIRICAL AND NON-EMPIRICAL STUDIES

philosophy
sociology
Enquiries
into
the problems of living and growing in society
(under the guidance of a class tutor)

NOTE
'Mixed questions' such as those described in Section 4 would be appropriate for discussions conducted by the class tutor: for example, questions which require a wide-ranging view of the humanities and/or the sciences.
Questions of this type may be thought of, at present, as part of the province of social studies, general science and liberal studies.

The sciences and geography are capable of developing in children an understanding of empirical and investigatory ways of asking and answering questions about the human environment; and history, anthropology, economics and psychology can fulfil a similar purpose in the study of human events and human behaviour. The other non-empirical studies, mathematics and languages (including a study of their own language), can help young people to develop an analytical approach to problem-solving and a capacity to make statements with precision and clarity. Young people should be able to discuss the activities offered with members of the staff and select a programme which will best meet their needs. For the teachers or counsellors who advise pupils the overriding criterion should be, 'Can the work be made relevant to their individual and social growth?'

Clearly there is considerable overlap between the lists of subjects outlined above and there is a case for suggesting that a study in depth of any human activity can lead, in part at least, to the development of the skills and attitudes associated with all modes of enquiry. However, it is also clear that some disciplines more readily illustrate certain methods of enquiry than others. The counsellor who wishes to help the individual pupil to choose a balanced course should make sure that it embraces the principal methods of enquiry. A course consisting of physics, French, pottery and history could probably as readily achieve the ends suggested in this report as one in literature, mathematics, anthropology and engineering.

Some people may regard such courses as narrow and undesirably specialised but, if the enquiries made are representative and are used for answering 'mixed questions' in the presence of a tutor, they could lead to effective ways of exploring a very wide range of experiences. At present we seem committed to the proposition that competent decisions are made by those who possess a wide general knowledge; hence the quest for a general education. This report, however, has argued that learning is not an end but a process—a way of understanding. Those who emerge as competent decision-makers should possess a broad understanding of ways of enquiring. The aim is the development of an education which is *general only in the sense that it gives young people a range of skills and attitudes which will allow them to understand themselves and their environment.* The successful student is not cheated because he has not been taught geography or science. If he needs to use these areas of knowledge for problem-solving he will have the skills which will enable him to recognise the value of the 'truths' in them. There is no final value in any particular field of knowledge; there is, however, the greatest value in the ways certain groups of disciplines ask questions and set about finding answers to them.

Engagement

> 1. *Do children feel that they are engaged in the work of the curriculum rather than 'learning about it'?*
> 2. *Do they find their work rewarding?*

The committee's contributions to these two questions have been discussed above in Section 4, 'Learning and Enquiry'. If all activities are genuine enquiries, structured for the growth of young people, there is little doubt that their curiosity will be tapped and their satisfaction assured.

Life-long Learning

> *Does the curriculum contribute to life-long learning?*

Life-long learning will only appear important to young adults if they have found their school experience stimulating and satisfying. If the school has helped them to live richer lives while they are studying, there will be no question of their rejecting the activities they have been engaged in. The degree of survival of interests generated in school will inevitably depend on the extent to which they have become a permanent part of a young person's behaviour.

'Vocational' Education

> *Does the curriculum prepare children to earn a living in adult society?*

This report has not attempted to separate learning into 'vocational' and 'non-vocational' compartments. Underlying the committee's thinking has been the tacit assumption that if young people learn and grow to the fullest extent of their capacities while at school, they will be well equipped to undertake training for a vocation when they leave school.

Any education designed to develop positive attitudes towards change must acknowledge that the qualities needed for success in a chosen vocation consist of more than technical skills (important as these are); personal qualities are also significant. From the United States it is reported that 'more employees are discharged for failure in human relations than for technical incompetence'.[9] In wealthy industrial nations 'life adjustment' has become extremely important in holding and advancing in a job. It is therefore reasonable to argue that 'education for living' is the most valuable aspect of 'vocational training' and that the most convenient agency for such education is the school system. Specialised training for a livelihood can then be given at tertiary institutions to young people who will more readily adapt to changing conditions and requirements.

Finally, it cannot be taken for granted that 'having a job' will be as important in the future as it is today. The ability to be 'fully human' will be a necessary attribute of a successful citizen in a community in which the time spent at work is dramatically reduced. This attribute will be developed only if our education system can help all young people to live full lives outside working hours. The teachers of so-called 'vocational' courses, for example, homecraft and technical, fill an important role here. Most if not all of these teachers see their activities as fully educational in the sense of contributing to their pupils' developing humanity. 'Artistic', 'recreational' and 'educational' would be apter terms for the work they do. In a modern educational system there is little place for the traditional view that the function of these studies is to impart actual job skills. Such preparation is the province of tertiary institutions and 'in plant' training.[10]

Resources

Will children have appropriate resources to work on and with?

Although this is the last question asked of the curriculum, it is by no means the least important. The other questions are searching for answers about effective learning. This last one is really about whether learning will take place at all. If the range of learning resources discussed in many sections of this report is not available, the chances of attaining desirable ends are very much reduced.

The relationship between a teacher and his class is in the truest sense the most important educational resource. If this relationship is endangered by giving the teacher too many pupils to work with, the quality of learning is decreased more rapidly than by any other cause.[11] Ideally no class should have more than twenty pupils and provision should be made for smaller tutorial groups and for individual tuition. Larger groups might be an advantage for films, television courses and lectures, but the basic working group should be small enough to make fruitful group-learning possible.

The physical environment of a school should reflect the kind of learning which is expected to take place within it. The 'institutional' appearance of even our newest schools suggests the cellular nature of the learning within them. If young people are to appreciate the significant relations between disciplines, artificial cell walls must be broken down. Our present school designs also reflect a serious lack of variety in the education itself. Schools lack rooms for private study, seminars and tutorials, and few have resource centres or well-equipped areas for relaxation and recreation. Schools with a wide range of working spaces and facilities would demonstrate our concern for children's diverse needs and for the various modes of teaching and learning that are available to us.

As well as being educationally effective, the environment should be planned to encourage young people's developing aesthetic values. The general appearance of our schools, their furnishing, fittings, lighting and decor have a significant effect on the taste of many young people. Too often our school designs have taken little account of pupils' aesthetic growth. Although many incorporate contemporary architectural features, impermanent materials have led to their rapid degeneration. Unattractive and uninspiring facilities do nothing to encourage children to place a fitting value on education.

The Curriculum in Action

This report has not aimed at producing a curriculum primer. It has asked questions and made some tentative explorations in seeking answers to them. Throughout, its concern has been child growth and the curriculum has been approached as a vehicle which can help in the realisation of certain desirable ends. Implicit in this view of the curriculum is the belief that ultimately it is the teacher who must set the goals and play the major role in establishing an environment in which learning can take place.

Teachers who work with a specific discipline must therefore have a deep knowledge and understanding of their special field of study.[12] They must, in short, *be enquirers themselves*. If they are less than this they may become competent instructors yet fail to establish conditions in which young people can enquire. When children are merely *told* about the knowledge and interests in a subject, they cannot develop the skills and attitudes which will allow their learning to become part of their own behaviour.

Teachers trained to understand the nature of child growth and the value of their own disciplines should be able to develop programmes of work which are appropriate to the young people in their classes.[13] Their insights should help young people to begin to generate their own learning and eventually make them capable of directing their own growth at all times.

There is little doubt that teachers cannot fulfil the fully creative role outlined in this report if they have limited time during the school day to organise their programmes, design and mark tests and assignments, and keep abreast of developments and research in their field. Their effectiveness is also reduced if their energies are taken up with matters not directly concerned with the education of children. If the talents of trained teachers are to be fully utilised, they should spend no more than half the school week with classes and their only clerical duties should be those which cannot be carried out by ancillary staff.

A Synthesis of Conflicting Aims

Throughout this section on the curriculum the committee believes it has squarely met the contrary demands of a specialist approach and a 'generalist' approach to schooling. A synthesis has been made which satisfies contemporary demands for the learning of disciplines and the ever-present need for individuals to have ways of solving the broad problems that confront them. The first demand can be met through the study of a balanced course of enquiries which accepts the criteria of this section, and the second through opportunities offered in tutor-seminars. General core approaches which have set out to help young people relate their knowledge have not always been successful because of the dearth of concepts and enquiry skills they have brought to problem-solving. However, if children pursue representative disciplines in depth they will be able to bring appropriate skills to bear in the presence of a tutor.

The synthesis outlined above would allow our schools to face the greatest challenge of our times: to provide for the 'implosion' of knowledge; to develop in young people the intellectual and creative capacities to use their learnings *for themselves*, to help them to order their knowledge and to encourage them to make sense of and be sympathetic to a wide range of human activities.

NOTE

A sequel to this report, which will include the 'minutes of evidence' of the committee's work, will illustrate approaches to a number of specific areas of the curriculum. The illustrations will not be schemes of work but will take the form of discussions about the most useful means of attaining specific goals within the subject areas selected.

SUMMARY OF SECTION [6]

The Balanced Curriculum

Educational Aims (summarised)

1. To help young people to acquire values which will aid their individual growth and social consciousness.
2. To develop their capacity to enquire in representative fields of study.
3. To develop their ability to relate the parts of their educational experience so that they can see this experience as relevant to their lives.

Relating Experiences

Young people must be given frequent opportunities to apply their total school experience to solving problems and answering questions that are of vital importance in their own lives.

Class Tutors (or teacher teams)

In order to help young people to relate their experience a new kind of teacher must be trained. His function would not be to provide children with answers but to help them to enquire with all their cognitive skills.

Teachers as an Educational Team

In our present situation, with schools staffed by specialists, the first necessity for achieving the objective of relating knowledge is to develop a total team approach. That is, all teachers should be required to work together in such a way that they begin to understand and appreciate the contribution each is making to children's education. This could not be done unless the school was conscious of its aims and all staff members were committed to their attainment.

Curriculum criteria that emerge from an understanding of the learning process

The following questions must be asked of the whole curriculum and of individual disciplines.

PSYCHOLOGICAL NEEDS

Will the curriculum facilitate the adjustment of young people to the school community and to society?

ORGANISATION FOR LEARNING

READINESS

Is the curriculum sensitive to the readiness for learning of children of differing abilities?

STRUCTURE
1. Does each discipline include the basic concepts which give it order and meaning?
2. Can the content material be organised so that effective learning is possible?
3. Does each succeeding period of study build on the ideas, skills, values, interests and attitudes of previous learning?

PROBLEM SOLVING:

Will pupils learn
1. to understand and to ask the kinds of questions appropriate to each area of study?
2. to use the procedures needed to find answers to these questions?

RELEVANCE

Is the curriculum relevant to the needs of society and to the pupils' individual and social needs?

EVALUATION
1. Does the curriculum provide for adequate teacher evaluation of pupil growth?
2. Does it help children to evaluate their own progress?

OPPORTUNITIES FOR LEARNING

PRACTICE

Does the curriculum give practice in representative modes of enquiry?

ENGAGEMENT
1. Do children feel that they are engaged in the work of the curriculum rather than 'learning about it'?
2. Do they find their work rewarding?

LIFE-LONG LEARNING
Does the curriculum contribute to life-long learning?
'VOCATIONAL' EDUCATION
Does the curriculum prepare children to earn a living in adult society?
RESOURCES
Will children have appropriate resources to work on and with?

The Curriculum in Action

1. It is the teacher who must set specific objectives for his pupils and play the major role in establishing an environment in which learning can take place.
2. Teachers must be enquirers themselves. If they are less than this, they may become competent instructors, yet fail to develop the conditions for enquiry.
3. Teachers trained to understand the nature of child growth and the value of their own disciplines can help children to generate their own learning and eventually develop a capacity to direct their own growth at all times.

[7] Interaction between School and Community

What is the function of education in a changing society? Potentially our schools are among the most powerful agencies for helping young people to revalue and better our society, but they cannot begin these tasks without widespread support from the community. A new trust is needed between the schools and the community; one which will encourage schools to re-examine their practices and seek ways of helping young people to enquire deeply into the purposes of our society.

This report has attempted to identify some needs of young people for the future and to see these needs against a background of change and in relation to present practices in our schools. It is evident to the committee that present practices are ill-matched to future needs.[1] The need to live with change and uncertainty, to face them with open and flexible minds, the need to be capable of making value judgements based on a deep understanding of personal and social behaviour—these are not being satisfied in our schools today.[2] Our practices, inherited from nineteenth-century British schools and directed towards training young people to fit into an unchanging social structure, are not only no longer useful, they are dangerous. New practices must be found if young people are to face the future with assurance.

Teacher-Parent Seminars

If innovations in our schools are to be of immediate value to young people a closer relationship must be established between parents and teachers. Closer ties cannot be created, however, merely by lecturing to parents on 'new' educational practices, for this often tends to make them feel more hopeless about the differences between their own education and their children's. Seminars and workshop sessions, in which parents actually participate in the new learning, are far more effective.

Here, of course, one comes up against the difficulty of adult pride. Can parents become sufficiently humble to be willing to try to understand the work their children are engaged in? False pride could be more readily overcome if the community were encouraged to regard learning as a life-long and continuous process rather than as one which ends with formal schooling. If parents began to look at learning in this way many of them could come to enjoy the opportunity of keeping abreast of contemporary learning, especially as they could build on a wider experience than their children possess. Parents who could accept their own need for further growth would also remain the intellectual and social contemporaries of their children.

'Parents must be respected because they are older and more experienced' is an age-old adage, but should this respect stem from the actual qualities of parents as civilised and educated individuals or should it accrue as an unchallengeable right? Much family conflict today arises when young people challenge their parents' beliefs and are answered not with argument but with dogmatic assertions.[3] Such dogmas have often been uncritically accepted by the parents in their own youth and contribute nothing to the solution of the problems of young people living in the present. Parents can aid their children to solve contemporary problems only if they are sensitive to change and to the needs which generate their children's questions, and if they constantly revalue their own attitudes.

Teachers are in a good position to identify young people's needs as they arise. They could therefore contribute to fruitful group discussion with parents about their understanding of these needs, provided there were real opportunities and facilities for such discussion. The group tutor envisaged by this report would be well placed to arrange worth-while informal discussions with parents about their children's more pressing needs. In such small informal groups tutors could learn to understand the parents' viewpoint better and parents could come to appreciate the schools' objectives.[4]

The Publication of Pupil Enquiries

Mutual understanding between school and community would be helped if some of the children's enquiries were made available to the public through the press, radio and television. Certain work done in our schools is worthy of display or publication (not only work in art and craft which is familiar enough to the public, but also children's findings in geography, ecology, sociology and other disciplines). This would give adults an opportunity to sample the work of the schools and to judge its worth for themselves. The selection of material would need to be by random sampling procedures rather than by competition because the public would learn nothing about the children's typical activities and achievements if publication and display were associated with rewards or prizes.

The Publication of Test Questions and Responses

Additional publications could well be made in the field of tests and examinations. Typical questions set in schools throughout the country could be periodically published, together with a wide range of responses. This would give adults a chance to understand the nature of the problems children face at various levels of their schooling. Such publications need not be over-technical and questions could be chosen which could be readily appreciated by adults.[5] Questions and some details of the marking procedures used, would help inform the public of the ways in which success was being measured. Parents should also be entitled to receive an outline of the purposes of public examinations and of the examiners' assessment of marker reliability and the validity of the measurements.

Community Influence on the Schools

The interchange of ideas between the schools and the community should be a steady dialogue. The community can influence the work of the schools in many ways and it can enrich children's learning. Again suitable avenues must be opened for this interchange. The present practice of having guest speakers to address school assemblies would hardly be appropriate in an educational system which placed a premium on discussion. Visitors with specialised knowledge should be encouraged to meet pupils in small groups so that they can be questioned directly and take part in discussion with them. Visitors from industry and public and professional life who are prepared for frank and probing questions can give young people an opportunity of finding out something of what is happening in the adult world and so help them to determine for themselves the skills and attitudes possessed by men and women in various occupations.

The community can also provide the schools with contemporary information. Reports from industry, government departments and research workers in many fields could be made available in sufficient quantities to enable young people to study their own society with the most recent data.

Finally the community can provide facilities which will allow children to see the working of the adult world at first-hand. Field trips have been popular for many years and some industries and institutions have encouraged visits by school parties. But there is a great need for more opportunities to be provided. Many field trips fail to help children's enquiries because they are presented merely as spectacles and the children are not encouraged to understand the methods and the purposes of the activity. Children's learning could be enriched if the hosts to school parties were to appoint permanent educational liaison officers (as some museums already do) and if the methods of enquiry used on field trips paralleled those advocated for in-school studies in Section 4 of this report.[6]

The Contribution of Parents to the Problems of Learning

There is a constant need for adults to participate in enquiries into learning itself. By doing so they would contribute directly to the work of the schools. This does not mean that parents should tell the schools what to do, any more than schools should dictate to the community. Both groups, teachers and members of the public, should work in partnership in order to contribute to young people's growth.

Schools and parents could work together most fruitfully in parent-teacher associations whose primary purpose was to explore the most acceptable ways of educating young people. Such associations should be seen as having a significance well beyond their present predominantly fund-raising activities. They could become valuable research groups concerned to test hypotheses about learning itself. For example the question:
'*Should all children be taught the detailed technology of modern machines?*'
could lead to a number of hypotheses which could be investigated by teams of parents working with teachers, notably:
Do children show a sustained interest in the details of modern appliances?
When children work with materials that are familiar in their home lives, do they find the learning more absorbing?
What aspects of the study of modern technology can lead children to ask more questions about their environment?

These and many other questions have not been tested in our own communities. Many parents and certainly many teachers would claim to know the answers to questions of this kind, but until data has been collected by questioning and observation our conclusions remain mere speculations. Many such speculations about the processes of learning have been accepted or rejected in the last decade as a result of careful research. As parents are in an excellent position to collect data about their children's behaviour they should be able to contribute significantly to an understanding of learning. Parents involved in enquiries about their children's growth would learn more about adolescent behaviour and also be likely to appreciate the need for constant experiment and change in our educational system.

SUMMARY OF SECTION [7]

New Communications

The school is potentially one of the most powerful agencies helping young people to revalue and better our society.

Teacher-Parent Seminars

1. Seminars and workshop sessions in which parents actually participate in new learning programmes are preferable to lectures about them.
2. If learning is seen as a continuous lifelong process more parents are likely to want to keep abreast of contemporary learning.
3. The group tutor would be well placed to arrange worth-while informal discussions with parents about their children's more pressing needs.

The Publication of Pupil Enquiries

Work done in our schools is worthy of display or publication (not only work in art and crafts, but also children's findings in geography, ecology, sociology and other disciplines). This would give adults an opportunity to sample the work of the schools and to judge its worth.

The Publication of Test Questions and Responses

1. Typical questions set in schools throughout the country and a typical range of responses could be published periodically, thus giving adults a chance to understand the nature of the problems children face.

2. Parents should also be entitled to receive an outline of the purposes of public examinations and of the examiners' assessment of marker reliability and the validity of the measurements used.

Community Influence on the Schools

1. Visitors with specialised knowledge should be encouraged to meet pupils in small groups so that they can be questioned directly and take part in discussion with them.
2. Children's learning would be enriched if the industrial and professional hosts to school parties were to appoint permanent educational liaison officers.

The Contribution of Parents to the Problems of Learning

1. Schools and parents could work together most fruitfully in parent-teacher associations whose primary purpose was to explore the most acceptable ways of educating young people.
2. These associations could also become valuable research groups concerned to test hypotheses about learning itself.
3. Parents involved in enquiries about the growth of their children would better understand the need for constant experiment and change in our educational system.

Conclusion

In its discussion of the purposes of education this report has made its own frame of reference and worked within it to explore the possibilities of fostering growth in young people. It has not sought to document all aspects of education and has tended to avoid detailed comment on political issues. For example, it has made no specific mention of the disputes about co-educational and single-sex schools, corporal punishment, school uniforms, state aid to private schools or the teacher shortage. These omissions are deliberate. The attitudes of the committee towards these questions can be inferred from the main arguments set out in the report, but if it had spent time in debating such questions it would have failed in its primary purpose—to make an unprejudiced exploration of the growth of children, and to direct attention to fresh ways of looking at their growth.

The report has also given little direct attention to the special problems of 'the slow learner', Maori and Pacific Island children and emotionally disturbed children in need of counselling. The committee has been very much aware of these problems but has approached them through discussion of desirable practices for *all* children instead of by singling out these groups for special attention. Preventive rather than therapeutic solutions have been sought. Education has been viewed in terms of positive practices for future growth rather than in terms of remedies for present failures. There is no doubt that our system has failed the less successful children, the children of Maori and Island parents and the emotionally disturbed. But perhaps before our schools attack these problems with remedial measures, our educational authorities should determine whether the schools are themselves accentuating failure through a lack of insight into their functions.

For its own part, the committee believes that optimum conditions for learning will not be attained in our schools unless there is a continuing enquiry into children's needs and the processes of learning. Contemporary research suggests that we have barely begun to understand the nature of human growth. Experimentation is in its infancy. However, there is increasing evidence throughout the world that the results of educational research are now keenly looked for and are being used to increase the effectiveness of learning.

This report makes its only formal recommendation in the area of experimentation and research. It is:

That, as the future of education in New Zealand will depend directly on the quality of experimentation, every encouragement

CONCLUSION 81

should be given to research conducted jointly by the schools and such professional bodies as the Curriculum Development Unit, The Council for Educational Research, the universities and the teachers' colleges.

The findings of many overseas experiments have been cited in this report, but it is the committee's intention that they should act only as guidelines for future experimentation in New Zealand. The findings of overseas research will not persuade many teachers to change accepted practices. If teachers were engaged in research enterprises themselves, however, it is possible that some would recognise new problems and look for fresh solutions. Change will not come about by directing our schools to alter their practices. Only if more of the general public as well as teachers can be involved in the business of learning about learning shall we grow above the level of our present ignorance.

NOTES ON SECTION [3]

1. 'The truest, healthiest incentive to learn lies within us and is spontaneous. Wrong ideas about what and how children should learn have made schoolmasters in the dark ages of education resort to the crude incentives of force. Less brutal but still damaging are many incentives practised today: rewards for the minority which are exclusive, carrying rejection for the unselected (e.g. prizes, prefect badges, comparative marks, ranking orders), and punishments which are no more than penalties, doing nothing to put the offender on a better path. . . .'
Robin Pedley, *The Comprehensive School.* 1963, p. 121.

2. L. J. Cronbach notes several principles of good motivation:
'Every activity should lead towards goals that the pupils are aware of and will want to attain.
'Goals should be within the pupils' reach, and should seem attainable to them.
'The pupils should be able to judge whether or not they are attaining their goals and how they are falling short.
'Classroom activities should lead to satisfactions that pupils will also seek outside the classroom so that the learned actions will be used in non-school situations.' *Educational Psychology* 1963, pp. 525-6.

3. 'Suppose that through intense social scholarship tightly integrated with sound creative research, the public school institution secured a fresh grasp of its total responsibilities so such things as the drop-out problem, the problems of mis-education and under-education are diminished to the smallest humanly possible dimensions; that through creative means a relationship between the public school institution, labour and industry becomes so strong and so

operative that the entire question of continuous training resolved itself. Suppose, in short, that the public school institution, through its own capacity for its own intellectual motivation became culturally, socially and creatively responsible, became, in point of fact, educational in its function. . . .

'Assuming all this, the question now develops as to the kind of personality the public school institution will turn out. *The answer is that he will be dissatisfied and hungry.** He will be dissatisfied with his present state of adulthood and hungry for the creative, dynamic experiences which will provide him, a living thinking entity, with vital opportunities for further personal growth and development in concert with a society struggling to civilize itself. He will be an individual who understands intrinsically that no matter what his achievement in promoting his own adulthood, that achievement will itself promote more dissatisfaction and generate an even more insistent hunger for more growth and development; that personal growth and development is, in fact, the process of becoming an adult. He will know that it is a process which only stops the moment he stops breathing. He will never be convinced that he has "arrived" anywhere no matter what evidence society gives him to the contrary. His sense of becoming will always be acute. His arriving will always be a departure, and a departure will always be an arriving.'
M. E. La Fountaine, *Continuous Learning.* Vol. 5, No. 1 (1966).

4. 'The elimination of economic insecurity was pioneered by the business firm in respect of its own operations. The greatest source of insecurity, as noted, lay in competition and the free and unpredictable movement of competitive market prices. From the very beginning of modern capitalist society, businessmen have addressed themselves to the elimination or mitigation of this source of insecurity. Monopoly or full control of supply and hence of price, by a single firm was the ultimate security.'
J. K. Galbraith, *The Affluent Society.* 1958, p. 90.

5. 'Evaluation in terms of improvement from one test to a later equivalent test guarantees that most pupils receive a favourable report most of the time. When each week's measure is in terms of the percentage of answers correct, with each test moving on to new material, the pupil has little sense of growth; he comes to think of himself as consistently pegged around 75 per cent, or some other level. A grade that compares him with others is equally uninspiring. Most of the class will be in the average range, passable but not distinguished enough to generate enthusiasm. Average though he may be, the golfer can be highly enthusiastic when he lowers his score from 100 to 90. School evaluation should make progress equally exciting for the pupil, but it rarely does.'
L. J. Cronbach, *Educational Psychology.* 1963, p. 553.

6. The only place for 'competition' is in friendly rivalry, which may sometimes be an aid to co-operative effort.

7. Finally, a word about one last intrinsic motive that bears closely upon the will to learn. Perhaps it should be called reciprocity. For it involves a deep human need to respond to others and to operate jointly with them toward an objective. One of the important insights of modern zoology is the importance of this intraspecies reciprocity for the survival of individual members of the species. . . .

'Probably it is the basis of human society, this response through reciprocity to

---

* The committee's italics.

other members of one's species. Where joint action is needed, where reciprocity is required for the group to attain an objective, then there seem to be processes that carry the individual along into learning, sweep him into a competence that is required in the setting of the group. We know precious little about this primitive motive to reciprocate, but what we do know is that it can furnish a driving force to learn as well.'
J. S. Bruner, *Toward a Theory of Instruction.* 1966, p. 125.

8. It is also true that most programmes can be adapted to the needs of almost any class group, provided the teacher understands the needs of his pupils and their readiness for learning. A programme which rapidly develops new skills can be adapted by varying the time spent at each level and by inventing new teaching situations which will aid the less successful pupils.

9. Independent study should not be thought of as taking place only in the pupils' own time. Ordinary class periods can often be used by children to carry through their investigations independently and in quiet secluded conditions.

10. McDonald (1961) reported studies by Latarjet in Vanves (France) and Stock in Brussels, in which academic studies were reduced by two or more hours a day, with a corresponding increase in the amount of time devoted to physical improvement in health and physical education. As would be expected a general improvement in physical fitness followed; however, there was also a corresponding increase in academic achievement. For example, the control group in the Vanves experiment attained 78 per cent in the elementary study certificate and the experimental group 84 per cent.

11. Rosenthal and Jacobson (1968) found that children whose teachers expected them to gain intellectually did, in fact, do so.
Their experiment consisted of casually advising teachers that certain children in their classes had done well in a new and unfamiliar (to the teachers) test of intelligence, and then post-testing all children in the classes four months and eight months later. *In fact the names passed on to the teachers had been selected at random. The difference between these children and those in the control group was entirely in the minds of the teachers.*
It was found that the children for whom intellectual growth was expected became more alive and autonomous intellectually, or at least were so perceived by their teachers. Overall, the results of the post-tests showed that children in the random experimental groups made greater gains in intelligence than those in the control groups. The gains were particularly marked among the younger children tested.
As there was no evidence that the pupils in the experimental groups had had special attention from their teachers, the investigators suggested that the teachers might have communicated their expectations to the pupils unwittingly: through tone of voice, facial expression, touch and posture.
A second finding suggested that teachers tended to regard unfavourably low-ability children whose intellectual growth had been marked (on the test evidence which was available only to the investigators). It seemed that teachers were unprepared to value unexpected growth in such children.
The experiment rested on the premise that at least some of the deficiencies in the growth of 'slow learners' — and therefore at least some of the remedies — might be in the schools and particularly in the attitudes of teachers towards such children.

12. Flynn and Munro (1968), in an experiment measuring the growth of problem-solving skills in science, found that there was no significant difference

between the gain scores of children in average streams and those in the top streams. This was in marked contrast to the opinions of the teachers who almost all suggested that the top streams had made significant gains while the average streams had failed to do so. It would seem that the teachers might have been evaluating growth in terms of knowledge gained rather than in terms of the skills measured, and were unaware of the true growth of the children's problem-solving abilities.

13. If no account is taken of children's differing rates of development an inflexible classification can lead to permanent masking of a child's ability.

14. 'Too often "intelligence" is thought of as something inborn and unchangeable, *whereas performance on these tests* (general tests of scholastic aptitude) *is substantially affected by experience.** We want to emphasize too that these tests stress abilities more relevant to the verbal, symbolic, convergent problems of the school than to other types of intelligent action.'
Educational Psychology, p. 203.

15. A finding of the Swedish experiment discussed below, note 16.

16. 'A recurring argument is that early transfer of talented pupils to separate classes or schools is essential if they are to make optimum educational progress. On this point we think the present study has some clear-cut answers to give.

(1) 'It made no difference in the long run to the achievements of plus-select pupils whether they received their prior instruction in one or other class-type. What superiority early-differentiated pupils may have enjoyed in their previous schooling had been reduced to practical nullity by the time all pupils reached grades 8 and 9.

(2) 'Over the long run, the placement of plus-select classes in State secondary schools, or both plus-selects and minus-selects in elementary and comprehensive schools, had no bearing on the achievements of pupils of comparable initial scholastic aptitude and home background.

(3) 'To minus-select pupils it was ultimately immaterial whether they were assigned to their respective classes early or late.

'It should once again be emphasized that our enquiries were confined to the scholastic attainments of pupils, which admittedly is a limited sector of the school's activities.'

Nils Eric Svenson, *Ability Grouping and Scholastic Achievement.* 1962, p. 176.

NOTE Plus-select classes are equivalent to academic classes in New Zealand. Minus-select classes are equivalent to non-academic or vocational classes in New Zealand.

17. 'High school grades, of course, indicate an ability to learn in particular learning situations only; such ability may include docility, lack of imagination, respect for an incompetent teacher, and other qualifications that a spirited and talented student may not possess. Finally, even if the correlation between the entrance battery of tests (including high school records) and College success is as high as .65, *58 per cent of the students will be misjudged and 12 per cent misjudged seriously.'**
Leod Nedelsky, *Science Teaching and Testing*, 1965, p. 186.

There is no reason to believe that present entrance tests to New Zealand secondary schools are any more successful at predicting student success. There

---

* The committee's italics.

CONCLUSION

is also good evidence to suggest that the measures made by our external examinations are also poor predictors.

18. e.g. Hillmorton High School
    Otumoetai College
    Timaru Girls' High School
    Waihi College
    Westlake Girls' High School.

19. A young person who has developed loyalty to a set of values, after a careful consideration of his own and others' behaviour, can remain flexible in his judgements providing he places the highest value on tolerance and is prepared to accept the right of others to attain 'the good life' by ways often quite different to his own.

NOTES ON SECTION [4]

1. B. S. Bloom, et al., pp. 201-4.
2. 'The action of art is to externalise the inner experience of man. This "externalisation" which occurs in ordinary speech can be raised to the level of metaphorical or symbolic expression when the nature of an experience denies a simple literal representation in words. Words are re-examined by the individual so that they will carry a new intensity or a new level of meaning and significance. This is the nature of the 'poetic' statement. Poetic should not be confused here with poetry. We *use* poetic statements in everyday affairs whenever we express how we feel about something. Metaphor has a special significance as a basic mode for the communication and expression of *values*. The more intense, the more significant the experience we wish to communicate, the more we depend on metaphorical speech or "art", and the more we must discriminate; the metaphor is not to be overgeneralised, bathetic or ambiguous. The search for precision in a statement is the economy of art.
'It is unfortunate that the presence of the action of "art" in our everyday communications is overshadowed and obscured by our rarification of the special arts, drama, poetry, pottery, etc. We tend, for example, to think of poetry as an art form separate from daily speech. It is really only a matter of degree. The child who says "I've had a few laughs, it's been good" is groping for a metaphorical level for the expression of his feelings — the result may be crude because the child has been encouraged to believe that poetry is special or "funny".
'The externalisation that occurs in the visual arts is of the same order and condition. Perhaps because of a time factor the person who externalises his experience in paint or clay searches himself in a private conversation to find the appropriate metaphor. This intense and apparently personal and private action which no one else can penetrate or participate in is always self-questioning. The performer, however, probably cannot verbalise the action which goes on in his self-examination. The person who is highly

---

* The committee's italics.

committed to his form of art (whether an "artist" or a pupil in school) inevitably comes to the humbling recognition of his own condition and the condition of others who are trying to solve similar problems.

'The social action of the art process will occur at two levels:
1. Personal self-scrutiny will lead to a respect for others who are engaged in similar self-scrutiny.
2. The expressive and communicative power of the art form itself is a social communication because we see something of the maker in what he makes.

'One of the very important aspects of art in a school situation is that valuable performances are not dependent on the experience or the age of the performer. A ten-year-old or a third former can produce something which has a recognisable value to a sixth former or an adult. Art does not historically evolve towards a better and better product; nor does art, in terms of personal growth, necessarily improve as a person grows older. Additional experience may enrich the quality of the product but does not guarantee a change in quality.'

B. P. F. Smith, Secondary Teachers' College, Auckland, 1968 (note provided for this report).

3. COMMON EXPERIENCE
   changes in the seasons
   shift from day to night
   living and dying
   eating and drinking
   losing and finding
   getting and giving
   standing still and moving about
   multiplicity of separate bodies that come to be and pass away
   change
   multiplicity of other persons with whom we communicate by language or other means
   pleasures and pains
   doubts and misgivings
   memories of the past
   anticipations of the future
   sensing and knowing
   sleeping, waking and dreaming
   growing and growing old

4. McKeachie (1964), in a review of college teaching, stresses the rough equivalence of lecture methods and discussion methods in inducing knowledge of subject-matter. However, he points out that courses using a problem-solving-discussion approach may excel lecture courses in producing skill in problem solving. The trends shown by McKeachie are in line with those shown by Stovall (1958). McKeachie makes the point that discussion is superior to lecture methods when the measures are other than final examinations testing knowledge.

Bloom (1953) found that discussion stimulated more active thinking than lectures did.

Dawson (1956) and Nedelsky (1965) have also stressed the effectiveness of discussion methods for achievement of goals other than the acquisition of information.

5. 'Brain research depends so directly on technical resources that its direction of development can be predicted from advances in physics and engineering. This is because there are almost no firmly established facts about brain function; everything remains to be discovered, all problems are still to be defined, every refinement of technique opens new possibilities of understanding and application.'
W. Grey Walter, *The Living Brain*. 1961, p. 11.

6. By Rogers (1956) and Piaget (1950).

7. Examples of tests are outlined in Section 5, p. 93, note 16.

8. 'It is likely that if enough tests were used, almost all children would be found to be *superior* in at least some area measured by the tests.'*
B. S. Bloom, 'Testing Cognitive Ability and Achievement', *Handbook of Research on Teaching*. 1964, p. 384.
'. . . any subject can be taught effectively in some intellectually honest form to any child at any stage of development.'
J. S. Bruner, *The Process of Education*. 1960, p. 33.

9. 'Growth depends upon internalising events into a "storage system" that corresponds to the environment. It is this system that makes possible the child's increasing ability to go beyond the information encountered on a single occasion. He does this by making predictions and extrapolations from his stored model of the world.'
Toward a Theory of Instruction. p. 5.

10. UNDERSTANDING.
Understanding implies the ability to use and apply knowledge and principles in unfamiliar situations. Examination questions which deal with content which has not been specifically covered in class give pupils the best opportunities of displaying this ability. If there is an attempt to measure 'understanding' in familiar situations the result may well be only an index of the ability to recall carefully memorised drills.

11. BEHAVIOURAL OBJECTIVES
There is a consensus among many educationists that statements of specific behaviours constitute the most useful way of expressing educational objectives.
The following authors have contributed to this consensus:
Gagné (1962); Aitkin (1968); Walbesser (1963); Walbesser (1966).

12. 'SOME OBJECTIVES AND BEHAVIOURAL CRITERIA IN SCIENCE

CATEGORIES	CRITERIA FOR A MARKING SCHEDULE
Skills and Abilities	
Comprehension and vocabulary	Evidence in the question that the meaning of the question has been conveyed.
Analysis and interpretation of data	Pupil judges relevance of data. Recognises trends. Avoids common errors in reasoning.
Extrapolation	Pupil cautiously argues beyond the presented data.

---

* The committee's italics.

CATEGORIES	CRITERIA FOR A MARKING SCHEDULE
Formulation of hypotheses, generalisations, explanations	Pupil formulates an hypothesis, explanation or generalisation which can be tested. Pupil points up ways in which the hypothesis can be tested.
Ability to devise experiments in order to test hypotheses.	Pupil shows what evidence is needed. Pupil shows the procedures for collecting the evidence.
Attitudes Accuracy (numerical and verbal)	Pupil shows accuracy of thought when reading question. Pupil is justifiably accurate in numerical work.
Intellectual honesty	Pupil gives his reasoning even though it seems contrary to accepted reasoning. Pupil willing to acknowledge ignorance.
Open mind	Pupil willing to abandon pre-determined ideas. Pupil accepts good evidence without arguing.
Critical mind	Pupil requests source of information. Pupil questions authority. Pupil questions validity of the information given.'

H. E. Flynn and R. G. Munro, 'Science Test Development Project', 1968.

13. ABILITY TO LEARN
'A student has an ability to learn if he is able to acquire knowledge and understanding of new material on his own. Learning from any kind of situation requires that the student be able to think in a disciplined and organised fashion; for example, his conclusions must correspond to the data. It may also require imagination; for example, the student may have to formulate searching questions about the situation or invent ways of modifying the situation experimentally.'
Science Teaching and Testing. p. 21.

14. Tentativeness has been a hallmark of sound learning and research throughout history. However, from the seventeenth to the twentieth century people thought that science was capable of arriving at certainties. In recent years this belief has been rejected and scientists have increasingly acknowledged the tentativeness of scientific conclusions. This revision of attitude was formalised in the 'Principle of Uncertainty' by the German physicist, W. Heisenberg (1927).

15. 'There is nothing more central to a discipline than its way of thinking. There is nothing more important in its teaching than to provide the child the earliest opportunity to learn that way of thinking — the forms of connection, the attitudes, hopes, jokes and frustrations that go with it. In a

CONCLUSION 89

word, the best introduction to a subject is the subject itself. At the very first breath, the young learner should, we think, be given a chance to solve problems, to conjecture, to quarrel, as these are done at the heart of the discipline.'
Toward a Theory of Instruction. p. 155.
16. This classification has been developed after referring, in particular, to the works of Hume (1711-1776) and Peterson (1960).
17. This phrase is discussed by Bruner (1956).
18. **Philosophical Questions**
      I THAT WHICH IS AND HAPPENS IN THE WORLD'
Nature of being and existence
properties of anything which is
modes of being — types of existence
change and permanence in being
existence of that which changes
change itself and types of change
causation and types of causes
necessity and contingency
material and immaterial
physical and non-physical
freedom and indeterminacy
powers of human mind
nature and extent of human knowledge
freedom of will
      II WHAT MEN SHOULD DO AND SEEK
            (ethical questions)
Human conduct and organisation of society
    good and evil
    right and wrong
    order of goods
    duties
    virtues and vices
    happiness
    life's purpose or goal
    justice and rights
The state and its relation to the individual
    the good society
    the just polity
    the just economy
    war and peace
      III MIXED QUESTIONS
        (including aspects of both questions I and II)
The ways in which we express our thoughts: language and questions about the content of our thinking.
(In these terms philosophy can be critical about its own thinking and usages and can provide accounts of other modes of enquiry.)

NOTES ON SECTION [5]

1. This way of thinking about education goes back at least to Tyler (1949).
2. Tyler (1934), Dressel (1949), Furst (1958), Elley (1967) and others.

There seems to be a consensus of opinion that evaluators should identify models and question types but that actual questions should be written by teachers and test specialists.
3. The evidence is that they are very poor instruments for this. Elley (1967).
4. **Effects of Examinations on Pupils, Teachers and Curricula.**
EXPERIMENTAL WORK
Merkhofer (1954) related the study behaviours of students to the comprehensive examination they were to take. He did this in terms of three different study behaviours. He found that the time spent on memorisation and re-reading of assignments, in contrast with that spent on applying ideas or methods, was related to the nature of the examination expected. Douglas and Tallmadge (1934) found that university students reported that they prepared for objective tests by focusing attention on minute details and the exact wording of books, but in preparing for free-response tests they favoured methods involving organisation of material, perceiving trends and relationships and the formation of personal opinions about the material. Meyer (1935) reported that university students tried to get a general picture of the material when preparing for essay tests but that they studied to learn details when preparing for objective tests.
In India Bloom (1964) reported that students resist learning not in harmony with external examination requirements.
It appears that students concentrate on preparing for the examination rather than on learning as such.
All India Council for Education (1958) reported that it was aware that teachers were under great pressure from pupils, parents and administrators to prepare pupils for the type of external examinations given.
5. POSITIVE VALUES OF TESTING AND EXAMINING
Examinations may have an important function in promoting learning. W. J. McKeachie writes: 'After dismal recitals of non-significant differences between different teaching methods it is refreshing to find positive results from variations in testing procedures.'
Research on Teaching at the University and College Level, 1964.
Jones (1923) found that immediate testing after a lecture improved retention. The good effects of the testing persisted or improved over an eight-week period.
Fitch, et al. (1951) found that pupils having weekly no-credit tests made better scores on monthly tests than an un-tested control group.
Maize (1954) at Purdue found that students who wrote forty themes individually and had them marked made greater improvement in a test of English usage than a group who had workbook drill and who wrote fourteen themes which were not marked.
Guetzkow, Kelly and McKeachie (1954) reported similar results.
May and Lumsdaine (1958) reported that learning from film is positively influenced by participation and feedback.
Stone (1955) in an Air Force experiment showed that performances benefited from the return of multiple-choice tests with information about the right and wrong responses. Five techniques were used ranging from simply giving raw scores to giving the fullest possible information. Giving full information proved superior to the other techniques.
Brian and Rugney (1956) found results in close agreement with those of Stone.
McKeachie and Hiler (1954) found that students evaluated on study questions performed better than students not given the questions, and also

tended to do better than students who were given the study questions, but did not have to hand them in for grading.

'Knowledge of results facilitates learning' is a generalisation then that has some foundation in research. It would appear that test feedback is one component of the optimum conditions of learning which lead one to 'learn how to learn'.

Kooker and Williams (1959) showed that pupils have limited insight into their own weaknesses and demonstrated the value of tests in helping to correct misinformation.

Plowman and Stroud (1942) arrived at similar results; so also did Kirkpatrick (1939) and Ross and Henry (1939).

Fitch et al. (1951) showed that merely giving tests has a motivating value and frequently a special value for weaker students.

Again we see that with adequate measurement of performance the pupil knows what he is accomplishing and what he has failed to grasp. Testing can help to direct effort as well as increase it. These principles apply of course to teaching-machine methods.

Cronbach (1963) and Keislar (1961) claim that evaluation can teach new ideas.

Further, Cronbach (1963) claims that non-test evaluations which are subjective can cause harm.

6. INSTRUCTION AND EVALUATION

Dressel (1954) has been a pioneer in helping teachers to see how instruction and evaluation are related. The following listing is his:

'Effective instruction leads to desired changes in the pupils.	Evaluation is effective as it produces evidence of growth.
'New behaviours are best learned when the inadequacy of present behaviours is understood.	Evaluation is most conducive to learning when it provides for and encourages self-evaluation.
'Teachers are more effective in bringing about behaviour changes when the existing behaviours and the reasons for them are known.	Evaluation is valuable when it points up inadequacies and their causes.
'Learning is encouraged by problems which require thought and activity on the part of each individual.	Evaluation is most significant in learning when it encourages the exercise of individual initiative.
'Activities that are most suitable for learning are also the most suitable for evaluating.	Activities or exercises developed for the purposes of evaluating a specified behaviour are also the most useful for the learning and teaching of that behaviour.'

P. L. Dressel, *Evaluation as Instruction*. 1954.

7. As a result of the research and writings of Tyler (1934, 1949), Furst (1958) and Dressel (1954).

8. Tyler (1934) produced evidence that the more complex objectives are retained longer than the simpler ones and that examinations after major units of work should test for this retention.

9. Adams (1964).

10. Flynn and Munro (1968)

11. This is all possible because of high correlations between the indirect (objective) and direct tests. It could be that pupils' study habits are

different when they expect objective tests from when they expect 'direct' tests. In this case the correlations mentioned may not remain high and after a time the objective tests may cease to be valid.

12. A COMPREHENSIVE EXAMINATION

A two-dimensional grid specification suggested by Adams (1964) is shown below:

OBJECTIVES COURSE CONTENT	Knowledge	Understand- ing Translation Interpretation Extrapolation	Application	Analysis
The gas laws	4	2	6	3
Spring of the air	2	1	4	4
Kinetic theory	5	4	4	2
Theory of the atom	2	4	3	3
Static electricity	4	4	4	2
Magnetism	5	2	3	3
Electricity and the nature of matter	3	3	6	3
TOTAL	25	20	30	20

G. S. Adams, *Measurement and Evaluation in Education, Psychology and Guidance*. 1964, p. 327.

Adams thinks that knowledge testing is more appropriate to teacher-made tests than to comprehensive examinations or standardised tests.

13. PRESCRIPTION FOR EXAMINATION. (One three-hour paper.)

'The examination will be set on the Syllabus in Science for Forms III-V. The syllabus indicates the content and general structure of the course and explanatory notes are provided to assist with the interpretation of the topics and to give a guide to the depth of treatment intended. In this form, the prescription should encourage the teaching of science based on an experimental and inductive method.

'OBJECTIVES

The objectives of the course are substantially the same as for Forms III and IV.

1. A knowledge of basic facts, principles and theories.
2. An understanding of fundamental concepts, and their application to new situations.
3. The application of scientific method: the ability to identify a problem, to bring to bear earlier experience relevant to the problem, to formulate explanations and hypotheses, to test by experiment or other means, to accept, modify or reject, and to draw conclusions.
4. The development of skills appropriate to science i.e., the ability to use scientific equipment accurately, to construct and interpret tables, charts and graphs, to find relevant information from reference sources.
5. The development of scientific attitudes such as openmindedness, intellectual honesty, a willingness to suspend judgment and a recognition of the tentative nature of theories.
6. A recognition of the importance of science in society.
7. The development of a continuing interest in science.

'EXAMINATION
In accordance with the objectives stated above, questions will, for the most part be designed to test:
1. Knowledge of basic facts, principles and theories. In this context knowledge means the ability to recall what has been taught in the course. It includes familiarity with experimental procedures and common apparatus.
2. Ability to use knowledge in familiar and unfamiliar situations and to apply scientific method to simple problems.
3. Appreciation of scientific attitudes and processes and their relevance to situations of social significance.

Approximately half of the marks in the examination will be allotted to questions testing the recall of knowledge, the other half to questions testing ability to use knowledge — with a small proportion to questions testing appreciation of scientific attitudes.

The examination will attempt to cover all sections of the syllabuses. Questions may be of objective or essay type as required.'
Science for Form V. Department of Education, Wellington, New Zealand, 1968, p. 2.

14. The College Entrance Examination Board in the United States issues a booklet of instruction and practice questions well in advance of the test. Such a booklet might well be amplified to help the candidate know how the examination will help him.

Hawkes et al. (1963) in *The Construction and Use of Achievement Examinations*, narrow all purposes of testing in schools to the single one of guidance of the pupil.

15. The effects of anxiety and fear of failure in any examination or test, the kinds of blockage and distorted responses that may result are discussed by Cronbach (1949). Again, he notes that placing the emphasis on the positive use of results to help the pupil is likely to improve the validity of the scores.

16. ACHIEVEMENT TESTS AT SECONDARY SCHOOL IN THE UNITED STATES.

The Co-operative Test Division of the Educational Testing Service fostered the development of end-of-course examinations in high school subjects. Subject-matter specialists in each high-school subject worked with test specialists in the construction of a large number of tests that would be acceptable to teachers.

There are comprehensive 80-minute tests for grades 7, 8, 9 on elementary algebra (beyond quadratics), intermediate algebra, plane trigonometry and solid geometry. In 1962 new tests in arithmetic, algebra and geometry were published. Additional tests in third-year algebra, trigonometry, analytical geometry and calculus were published in 1964.

There are science tests for grades 7, 8, 9 in general science, physics, chemistry and biology.

There are 80-minute tests for grades 7, 8, 9 in history, government, ancient history, modern history and world history. In the revised series published in 1965 for junior high school and senior high school there are tests in American history as well as revised tests in government, world history and modern European history.

Language tests now include one-period tests in French, Spanish, Latin. A listening comprehension test in French is also available.

A comprehensive testing programme covers:
1. Five languages.
2. Four skills in each language (reading, writing, history, speaking).
3. Two levels in each skill.
4. Two equivalent forms for each level.

This means some eighty new tests altogether. The series includes the first standardised tests ever developed of ability to speak foreign languages.

Another series, Evaluation and Adjustment Series, is published by Harcourt Brace and World Inc. This includes more than twenty subject-tests at high-school level, provides item norms and permits teachers to omit certain questions or make new combinations of some others. Another unusual feature is that by equating the average standard score on a physics test to the average I.Q. of physics students and making similar adjustments for other high-school subjects, a set of standard scores has been developed which is comparable from subject to subject. This makes comparisons between individuals possible and makes it easy to compare the achievement of individuals or groups with expected achievement.

These techniques help teachers to take advantage of professional item-writing without tailoring their teaching to tests; they help in individual and group diagnosis and help counselling and guidance services to the individual. The interpretation of the evidence from achievement tests involves knowledge of scholastic aptitudes. There are devices that help test users to modify their expectations for students whose I.Q. is considerably above or below average. Other information on school populations such as local language use and socio-economic status is needed before valid comparisons can be made between schools.

Many school districts in the United States administer a selected achievement battery of tests at several different grade levels as a basis for ascertaining growth. Here again differences of scholastic aptitude between classes need to be considered in assessing gains. Discussion of other important effects such as the 'regression' effect can be found in Adams (1964).

17. PUBLIC EXAMINATIONS IN NEW ZEALAND

An additional goal for examinations (School Certificate) is envisaged in the *Report of the Commission on Education in New Zealand,* 1962. The Commission believes that the School Certificate Examination is raising the cultural level of the community and seems quite prepared to accept tension and anxiety on the part of parents (and therefore children) because it is associated with this development.

The Commission realises that the public have been uneasy about scaling, which gives the Department of Education control over this examination, but asserts that the teaching profession largely agrees with the Department of Education's scaling policy.

In general it appears that the Commission views School Certificate as a satisfactory terminal course measuring a level of general educational attainment. Statements about the University Entrance Examination, based largely on Parkyn (1959), suggest that accrediting is no worse than an external examination and that university drop-outs result largely from factors over which the school has no control. The Commission seems to see university training as a different process from school education.

The Commission appears confused about examinations. The report asserts that examinations will be with us for a long time yet and says that an important function of the examination is to be a 'goal' — by this it means an 'end'. The report goes on to say that examinations help teachers to keep up with the growth of knowledge.

The report also notes that the subject specialisation characteristic of secondary schools is well served by examinations and that examinations thrive on specialisation.

The Commission considers it worth while preserving examinations for the reasons given. In discussing the dangers of external examinations, such as limiting subject content to the testable, they see the main ways of meeting these dangers as:

(a) Professional responsibility in the individual teacher.
(b) The services of teachers who are enthusiastic for their subjects and therefore willing to accept such responsibility.
(c) Guidance and direction of teachers by experienced principals and heads of departments.
(d) Involvement of teachers in the examinations themselves.

A final point made by the Commission is that many pupils are disappointed and frustrated by failing an examination they should never have taken.

18. '. . . there still persists an implicit belief that if cognitive objectives are developed, there will be a corresponding development of appropriate affective behaviours. Research summarized by Jacob (1957) raises serious questions about the tenability of this assumption. The evidence suggests that affective behaviours develop when appropriate learning experiences are provided for students much the same as cognitive behaviours develop from appropriate learning experiences.'

D. R. Krathwohl, et al., *Taxonomy of Educational Objectives*. Handbook II, 1964, p. 20.

19. ATTITUDE QUESTIONNAIRE

The following questionnaire from Nedelsky (1965), illustrates a useful method for making judgements about a pupil's attitudes and habits in science.

'MISCELLANEOUS ATTITUDES AND HABITS

Some of the statements below may be considered right by some people and wrong by others; therefore you are not asked to mark the statements true or false, but to give us your own point of view by writing (a) before the statement if you are inclined to agree with the main idea of the item, and (b) if you are inclined to disagree.

'Guessing of any kind or acting on a hunch should never be indulged in by a true scientist.

'A true scientist should not be concerned with increasing the accuracy of laboratory measurements from 1 per cent to .1 per cent, and so forth; he should devote his time to seeking after the larger truths of nature.

'The events in the lives of individuals can be predicted, in a general way, by the configuration of the planets and the moon at the time of birth.

'With further development of scientific thinking, we may discover certain facts about nature, which we shall not be able to test by observation or experiment.

'A real scientific genius can, without using any experimental data about matter, find out (by thinking) more about what atoms are really like than can an ordinary physicist by performing experiments.

'A clear scientific thinker could have become convinced without experimentation that a feather falls more slowly than a stone only because of the interference of air. He could have predicted with certainty that in a vacuum all bodies would fall with the same acceleration, that is, gain the same amount of speed in one second.

'Whatever scientists say about the inside of a star is really theorizing or speculation; they can never be sure about it.

'The action of a radio tube has been explained completely satisfactorily in terms of the motion of electrons. No one has been able to explain it in any other way. Therefore, electrons exist.

'If a scientist does his research into the nature of physical phenomena without being concerned how such knowledge can be applied practically, the chances that his discoveries will ever be useful in a practical sense are small.

'In science, as is true in all endeavours, certain statements have to be accepted as true because of the judgment of an authority, even though he cannot definitely prove them.

'Some of the scientific discoveries of recent years have led to misery and suffering. Humanity would in the long run be happier if such discoveries were never made.

'A photo-electric cell has been constructed on the theory that electrons exist. The theory explains the action of the cell very well, and the cell operates satisfactorily. What would be the proper course of action if in the future the scientists should decide that electrons do not exist?
(Mark *each* statement A or B.)
'We should stop using the photo-electric cell.
'We would have to reconstruct the cell.
'We could continue using the cell without changing it.
'We could continue using electronic theory in explaining the action of the cell.

'COMMENTS ON EXERCISES TESTING ATTITUDES AND HABITS

'It should be emphasized that these exercises will not justify an absolute judgment of the student's attitudes or habits but only a comparison with the group taking the test. One of the main reasons is the great difficulty of estimating the relative attractiveness of the wrong answers.'
Leo Nedelsky, *Science Teaching and Testing.* 1965, pp. 341-2.

INTERESTS

Most interest inventories make measurements in terms of likes and dislikes or preferences for particular inventoried interests. The low correlation between interests and aptitudes suggests that there is a significant difference between the two measures. Interests may affect the direction of effort, whereas abilities affect the level of achievement. Some factors may, however, mask the relationship; it is thought, for example, that personality factors play a part in the development of interests.

TYPES OF INTEREST AND ATTITUDE INVENTORY
1. Preference Type: Pupil scores indicate the extent of likes and dislikes for specific activities, subjects etc. Preferences are then summarised according to interest groups: clerical, scientific, technical etc.
2. Measures of Positive and Negative Attitudes:
Tests of the predisposition of pupils to act positively or negatively towards objects, classes of people, institutions etc. Pupils are then scored on a scale running from positive to negative.

CONCLUSION

3. Measures of Manifest Attitudes:
Attitudes such as 'scientific temper' are assessed by direct observation.

DIFFERENCES BETWEEN INTEREST AND ATTITUDE MEASURES
The major difference is found in the organisation of the items and interpretation of the responses. Both can look very much the same. Attitude questionnaires feature questions which are selected to represent a universe of attitudes and responses are recorded on a predetermined scale. Interest questionnaires, on the other hand, are designed so that a set of criteria can be applied to the responses.

ABILITY TO DEFEND ATTITUDES
A teacher may be interested in the ability of a pupil to defend his attitudes rather than in the attitudes held. Measures can be made of the ability of pupils to defend or describe their attitudes; such tests do not attempt to evaluate the attitudes held.

CHANGES IN ATTITUDE
It is possible to make group measurements of changes in attitude, but it is more difficult to establish reliable procedures for determining changes in individuals. A scale running from positive to negative is the most convenient to record such changes in groups.

ATTITUDE SCALES
Thurstone Scale: Positive and negative reactions to a large number of statements are obtained. Judges are then asked to indicate their view of each reaction in terms of an 11-point scale which runs from extremely favourable, through neutral to extremely unfavourable. Responses given various values by the judges are eliminated as ambiguous or unrelated to the attitudes being measured; only those with low interjudge variability are retained. Self-consistent sets of responses are accepted and twenty-five of the items are then selected for the test.
Likert Scale: Positive and negative reactions to statements are each ranked on a 5-point scale by a representative group. The scale ranges from 'strongly approved' through to 'strongly disapproved'. Only items which correlate highly with the total score are retained. The scale is established by setting the items to a representative population rather than to a set of judges.
The correlation between the two scales is .8. Both scales should be used with caution. Tests which summarise verbal statements by pupils are not necessarily indicators of their real attitudes and interests. However, the results can serve as useful guides to teachers.

PERSONALITY AND SOCIAL ADJUSTMENT MEASURES
Measures of mental health, maturity and social adjustment are of two kinds:
1. psychometric measures.
2. clinical measures used to diagnose suspected maladjustment.

Instruments used include: self-reports, questionnaires, inventories, autobiographies, direct observations of relevant behaviours, interviews, check lists and rating scales. Results are used to identify young people needing help because of their failure to relate to others in the school community.

20. *Taxonomy of Educational Objectives,* Handbook II, 1964.
21. Handbook I of the *Taxonomy* displays a continuum of cognitive objectives which range from the simple to the complex. The continuum set out in Handbook II, however, moves through affective objectives in the direction of increasing internalisation. The higher objectives here are associated with behaviours which have become a permanent part of the inner life of the individual.

INTERNALISATION
'. . . in the *Taxonomy* internalisation is viewed as a process through which there is at first an incomplete and tentative adoption of only the overt manifestations of the desired behaviour and later a more complete adoption.'
Handbook II, p. 29.
'At the lowest levels of the internalisation continuum there is little emotion in the behaviour. At this end the individual is mainly just perceiving the phenomenon. At the middle levels, emotional response is a recognised and critical part of the behaviour as the individual actively responds. As the behaviour becomes completely internalised and routine, this emotion decreases, and is not a regular part of most responses.
'Another aspect of the growth is the extent to which external control by the environment yields to inner control as one ascends the continuum. Thus at the lowest end of the continuum inner control serves only to direct attention. At higher levels, inner control produces appropriate responses, but only at the bidding of an external authority. At still higher levels, inner control produces the appropriate response even in the absence of an external authority. Indeed at still higher levels, these responses are produced consistently despite obstacles and barriers.'
Ibid, p. 30.

NOTES ON SECTION [6]

1. General questions which children could discuss in tutor or tutor-team sessions:
   1. Many of the broad problems which are associated with Social Studies and Liberal Studies courses and which impinge on children's own behaviour and concerns.
   2. The relationship of various discipline areas to current personal, community, national and international problems.
   3. The nature and causes of human behaviour.
   4. The purposes of schooling.
   5. Experiments in learning and theories of learning (studies of chimpanzees, dolphins etc.). Problem-solving in education.
   6. The nature of different kinds of knowledge and enquiry.
   7. The nature of 'proof' as it applies in different areas of endeavour.
   8. The nature of language and its effects on the acquisition of knowledge.
   9. The arts and sciences — are they the same or different? Goals and methods in the arts and the sciences.

SPECIFIC AREAS OF CONCERN
Urbanisation, conservation, mass media, traffic accidents, space exploration,

TUTOR SEMINARS

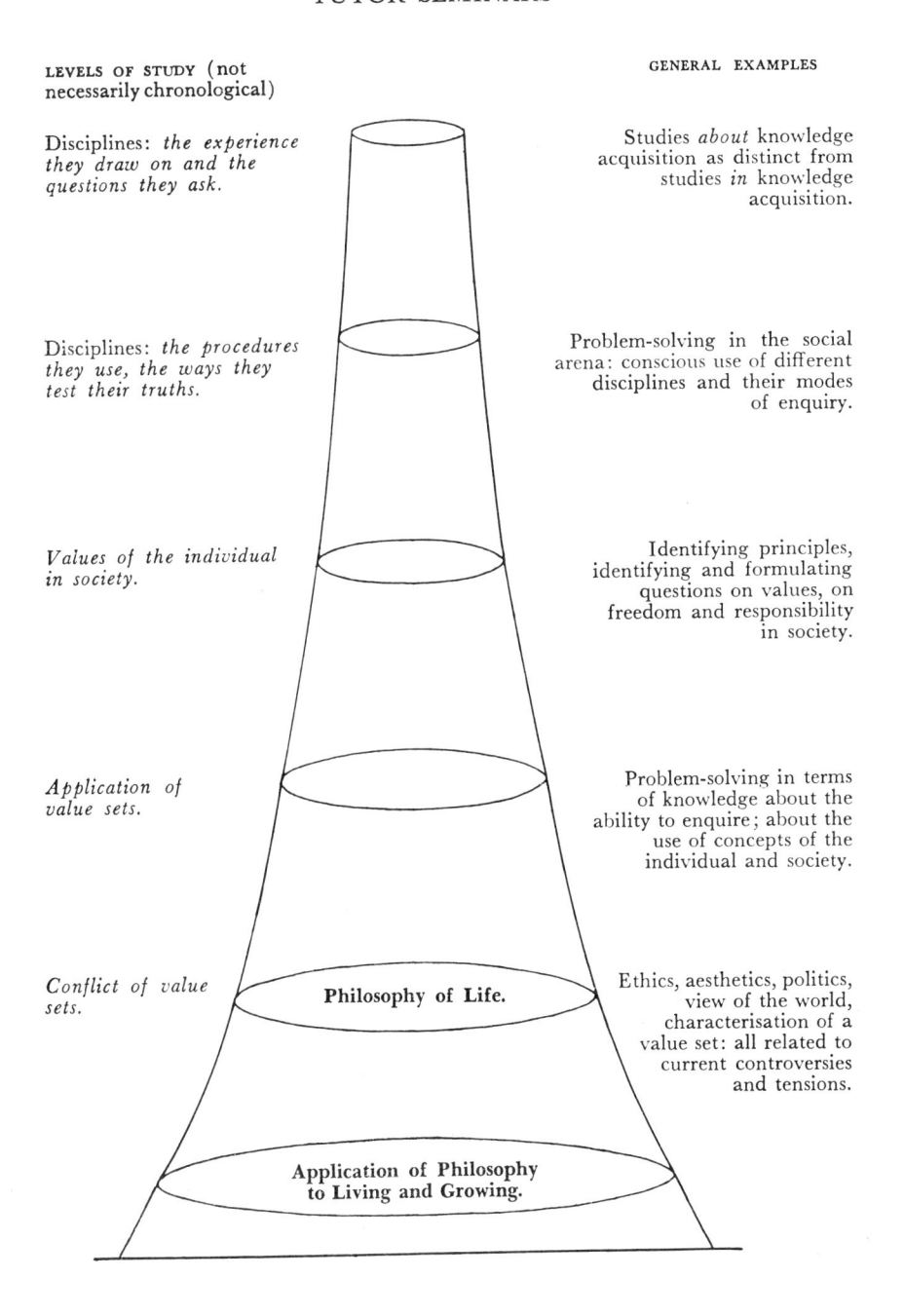

LEVELS OF STUDY (not necessarily chronological)		GENERAL EXAMPLES
Disciplines: *the experience they draw on and the questions they ask.*		Studies *about* knowledge acquisition as distinct from studies *in* knowledge acquisition.
Disciplines: *the procedures they use, the ways they test their truths.*		Problem-solving in the social arena: conscious use of different disciplines and their modes of enquiry.
Values of the individual in society.		Identifying principles, identifying and formulating questions on values, on freedom and responsibility in society.
Application of value sets.		Problem-solving in terms of knowledge about the ability to enquire; about the use of concepts of the individual and society.
Conflict of value sets.	**Philosophy of Life.**	Ethics, aesthetics, politics, view of the world, characterisation of a value set: all related to current controversies and tensions.
	Application of Philosophy to Living and Growing.	

technology, apathy, automation, leisure, fashion, personal tastes, boredom, growth, patriotism, famine, United Nations, peace, marriage, parenthood, strikes, unemployment, population explosion, contraceptive pill, Negro ghettos, Vietnam, Rhodesia, student riots, drugs, alcohol, apartheid, the arms race, ideologies.
(This list is not meant to be exhaustive; it is given only to illustrate possible areas for discussion.)

2. All children should be given opportunities to understand the value of statistical evidence, including problems of sampling and interpretation. They need this understanding in order to follow and to make judgements about statistical statements presented to them by the mass media.

3. Some of the major challenges for young people should arise through frustrations that are deliberately built into the processes of learning. Frustrations are important in the growth of individuals and schoolwork which is tidy and complete does not provide the kind of open-ended challenges which help children to grapple with ideas and synthesise their own solutions. Frustration can produce fresh and fruitful hypotheses during enquiries and creative acts in the arts. Classwork which makes no allowance for this stimulus to learning may fail to generate true involvement. The student who has investigated, for example, a particular model for explaining phenomena and has found it inadequate will find his explorations of a more useful model the more stimulating.

4. Bruner, in discussing the meaning of the word *curriculum*, sees education as continuous and not as terminal.
'. . . a word that derives from a course to be run. It is perhaps a wrong word. A curriculum should involve the mastery of skills that in turn lead to the mastery of still more powerful ones, the establishment of self-reward sequences. . . . The reward of deeper understanding is a more robust lure to effort than we have yet realised.'
Toward a Theory of Instruction, p. 35.

5. There are many 'structured' courses available which develop concepts in an order of increasing complexity.

6. 'Any discipline has three main elements.
    1. 'It has a domain — the phenomena, or aspects of life, for which it takes responsibility.
    2. 'It has methods or rules according to which the scholar in the discipline seeks out and handles the data given in the domain, and according to which the quality of the generalizations he reaches may be judged. Included in the method or the rules, is an agreement on the type of generalization or output appropriate to the discipline.
    3. 'Any discipline has a history, or a tradition, which enters into the decision on both the domain and the rules according to which it proceeds as a field of learning.'

A. W. Foshay, 'Discipline-centred Curriculum' in *Curriculum Crossroads*. 1962, p. 68.
Bellack, speaking of curriculum projects, notes:
'Their aim is to introduce students to the universe of discourse, or more grandly, the ways of life, represented by the fields of scholarship. Students are to engage in activities patterned after those of the practising physicist, chemist or economist. Whereas formerly factual and descriptive content of the various fields was stressed, now the emphasis is on basic concepts and

CONCLUSION

conceptual relationships that scholars in the various fields use as intellectual tools to analyse and order their data.'
A. Bellack, *The Nature of Knowledge.* 1962, p. 43.
7. Attempts to fabricate new disciplines out of sections selected from others have often failed because self-consistent structures have not been apparent. Some exercises in Social Studies, General Science and Liberal Studies are in this category.
8. *See above,* Section 4, Note 18, II.
9. G. T. Kowitz and N. G. Kowitz, *Operating Guidance Services for the Modern School.* 1968, p. 18.
10. 'Since then (1939) it has become generally accepted by economists that, for economic reasons, it is necessary in New Zealand that every child be given an education to the full extent of his powers and that any specialized training should be postponed until the broad education has taken place, partly because the broad education must not be skimped and partly because it is necessary to master new vocational techniques — very necessary if New Zealand is to survive with its western-type living standards.
'This view has, for example, become accepted by New Zealand Federated Farmers who prefer that those going into farming have a broad general education that does not include any pseudo-vocational specialization such as agriculture, but that agriculture be properly studied at a tertiary institution. Much the same view has been expressed by the education committee of the Wellington Chamber of Commerce which said that "a school leaver was a better employee if he had a good general education, rather than having the emphasis put too much on commercial or occupational trade subjects." '
(*Evening Post,* Wellington, 29 March, 1966.)
W. B. Sutch. *Plans Without Planning,* Inaugural Lecture. 'The J. T. Stewart Lecture on Planning', Palmerston North, 1967.
11. Surveys by teacher organisations in this country have also suggested that the large size of classes is forcing many able teachers to leave the education service.
12. The term 'discipline' has been preferred to 'subject' in this report. The word 'subject' is usually associated with the acquisition of knowledge; the richer implications of a discipline-approach to learning are discussed in Note 6 to the present section.
SUBJECTS AND DISCIPLINES
The following table illustrates the main differences between subject and discipline approaches to learning:

Subject-centred	Discipline-centred
1. Expects automatic transfer of training.	Accepts the possibility of transfer by assisting children to learn how to learn.
2. Believes that application produces achievement for all.	Recognises that there are different levels of achievement.
3. Emphasises preparation for adulthood.	Emphasises preparation for the present as well as the future.
4. Competitive rather than co-operative approach.	Opportunities for co-operation and contribution.
5. Stresses group learning and class standards.	Recognises individual differences and provides for individual as well as group learning.

Subject-centred	*Discipline-centred*
6. Assumes a hierarchy of difficulty of subject matter.	Assumes that children can learn concepts at an early age.
7. Stresses memorisation of facts.	Emphasises meaning and understanding of concepts involved and stresses understanding of the structure, purposes, methods and history of the disciplines studied.
8. Encourages textbook teaching.	Encourages discovery, experimentation, exploration, invention and the use of a variety of printed and audio-visual material.
9. Emphasises a logical approach to learning.	Approach depends upon the discipline studied (uses a logical approach where appropriate).
10. Gives little opportunity for creativity in learning.	Stresses the importance of creativity in learning.

13. The subject of teacher education will form the basis of a further study by the Curriculum Review Group.

NOTES ON SECTION [7]

1. 'The curriculum is retrospective in character at the expense of contemporary movements. It works from a well established traditional body of knowledge which is assumed to be of inherent value. The school is seen by society as a place where children are selected and prepared for the labour market. They are shaped in their formative years not according to their developmental needs, but so that they fit into pre-ordained niches. The pressures of parents, employers and universities constrict the school within a strait-jacket of examinations. Yet we have evidence from the same agencies that the products of the school disappoint. Small wonder when the system has extruded those who by sex or class prefer to opt out of this obstacle race and when the criteria for selection give credit to convergent thinking and a willingness to conform to conventional patterns of attainment.' *First Pilot Course for Experienced Teachers.* 1965, p. 56. (University of London.)

2. An analysis of our public examinations suggests that few thinking skills are being promoted by our schools and measured by our examinations. For example, very few of the questions set to children in the School Certificate, University Entrance, University Bursary or Scholarship examinations place children in unfamiliar situations which can test the openness or flexibility of their minds. This is very largely the result of an unwritten principle which many of our examiners adhere to far too narrowly: 'that no question should be set which is outside the prescribed syllabus.'

3. 'An imposed or even strongly recommended Christian or any other form of ethics has no relevance to our children or ourselves and any code of

behaviour which will have any permanence in the lives of the children we teach must be worked out, with helpful guidance, by themselves.'
Second Pilot Course for Experienced Teachers. 1965, p. 35. (University of London.)

4. The New Zealand survey of parent preferences in education, conducted by Robert Havighurst in 1954, offers good evidence that many parents welcome the opportunity to discuss the ends of education.

5. This communication with parents should also help them to understand the purposes of evaluation in the classroom. (See Section 5.) Parents often think of tests and examinations as measures of the effectiveness or ineffectiveness of teachers and teaching methods. Parents should somehow be led to understand the more important concept: that evaluative procedures can provide insights which help us improve education. If they can see good testing as a way of finding out more about learning itself they are likely to develop a richer appreciation of the purposes of good classroom tests and of the findings of educational research.

6. Such liaison officers should become much more than instructors. Through working closely with the schools they would become aware of the special needs of the children who visit them and adapt their programmes to suit, thus becoming educators in a full sense.

Bibliography

Adams, G. S. *Measurement and Evaluation in Education*. New York: Holt, Rinehart and Winston, 1964.
Aitkin, J. M. *Science Teacher*. (May 1968).
All India Council for Secondary Education. *Evaluation in Secondary Schools*. New Delhi, 1958.
Bellack, A. *The Nature of Knowledge*. Madison: University of Wisconsin Press, 1962.
Bloom, B. S. 'Thought Processes in Lectures and Discussion', *Journal of General Education*. 7, (1953).
Bloom, B. S. et al. *Taxonomy of Educational Objectives*, Handbook I, Cognitive Domain. New York: Longmans, 1956.
Bloom, B. S. 'Testing Cognitive Ability and Achievement', *Handbook of Research on Teaching*. N.L. Gage, ed., Stokie: Rand McNally, 1964.
Brian, G. L. and J. W. Rigney. *Electronics Personnel Research Group Technical Report 18*. Los Angeles: University of Southern California Press, 1956.
Bruner, J. S., et al. *A Study of Thinking*. New York: Wiley, 1956.
Bruner, J. S. *The Process of Education*. Cambridge: Harvard University Press, 1960.
Bruner, J. S. *Toward a Theory of Instruction*. Cambridge: Harvard University Press, 1966.
Cooperative Test Division. *Sequential Tests of Educational Progress*. Princeton, New Jersey: Educational Testing Service.
Commission on Education in New Zealand. *Report of the Commission on Education in New Zealand*, Wellington, 1962.
Cronbach, L. J. *Essentials of Psychological Testing*. New York: Harper, 1949.
Cronbach, L. J. *Educational Psychology*, 2nd ed. London: Rupert Hart-Davis, 1963.
Dawson, M. D. 'Lecture Versus Problem Solving', *Science Education*. 40, (1956).
Douglas, H. R. and M. Tallmadge. 'How University Students Prepare for New Types of Examination', *School and Society*. 39, (1934).
Dressel, P. L., et al. *Comprehensive Examinations in a Program of General Education*. East Lansing: Michigan State University Press, 1949.
Dressel, P. L. 'Evaluation as Instruction', *Proceedings, 1953 Invitational Conference on Testing Problems*. Princeton, New Jersey: Educational Testing Service, 1954.
Elley, W. B. 'Standardised Tests in New Zealand', *New Zealand Journal of Educational Studies*. Vol. 2, No. 1, (1967).

Evaluation and Adjustment Series. New York: Harcourt, Brace and World, 1966.
Fitch, M. L. et al. 'Frequent Testing as a Motivating Factor in Large Lecture Classes', *Journal of Educational Psychology.* 42, (1951).
Flynn, H. E., and R. G. Munro. 'Science Test Development Project.' Auckland, New Zealand, 1968. (unpublished)
Foshay, A. W. 'Discipline-Centred Curriculum', *Curriculum Crossroads.* New York: Teachers College, Columbia University Press, 1962.
Furst, E. J. *Constructing Evaluation Instruments.* New York: David McKay, 1958.
Gagné, R. M. 'The Acquisition of Knowledge', *Psychological Review.* 69, (1962).
Galbraith, J. K. *The Affluent Society.* Harmondsworth: Penguin Books, 1958.
Grey Walter, W. *The Living Brain.* Harmondsworth: Penguin Books, 1961.
Guetzkow, H., et al. 'An Experimental Comparison of Recitation, Discussion and Tutorial Methods', *Journal of Educational Psychology.* 45, (1954).
Havighurst, R. J. et al. *Studies of Children and Society in New Zealand.* Christchurch: Canterbury University College, 1954.
Hawkes, H. E. et al. *The Construction and Use of Achievement Examinations.* Boston: Houghton Mifflin, 1963.
Hume, D. (1711–1776). *Enquiry Concerning Human Understanding.*
Jones, H. E. 'Experimental Studies of College Teaching', *Archives of Psychology.* Vol. 10, No. 68, (1923).
Keislar, E. R., and J. D. McNeil 'Teaching Scientific Theory to First Grade Pupils by Auto-Instructional Device', *Harvard Educational Review.* 31, (1961).
Kirkpatrick, J. E. 'The Motivating Effect, of a Specific Type of Testing Program, *University of Iowa Studies in Education.* Vol. 9, No. 4, (1939).
Kooker, E. W., and C. S. Williams. 'College Students' Ability to Evaluate Their Performance on Objective Tests', *Journal of Educational Research.* 53, (1959).
Kowitz, G. T., and N. G. Kowitz. *Operating Guidance Services for the Modern School.* New York: Holt, Rinehart and Winston, 1968.
Krathwohl, D. R. et al. *Taxonomy of Educational Objectives*, Handbook II, Affective Domain. New York: David McKay, 1964.
La Fountaine, M. E. *Continuous Learning.* Vol. 5, No. 1, (1966).
McDonald, A. *New Zealand Journal of Physical Education.* Vol. 23, (April 1961).
McKeachie, W. J. and W. Hiler. 'The Problem—Oriented

Approach to Teaching Psychology', *Journal of Educational Psychology*. (1954).

McKeachie, W. J. 'Research on Teaching at the University and College Level', *Handbook of Research on Teaching*, M. L. Gage, ed., Stokie: Rand McNally, 1964.

Maize, R. C. 'Two Methods of Teaching English Composition to Retarded College Freshmen.' *Journal of Educational Psychology*. 45, (1954).

May, M. A., and A. A. Lumsdaine. *Learning from Films*. New Haven: Yale University Press, 1958.

Meyer, G. 'An Experimental Study of Old and New Types of Examinations', *Journal of Educational Psychology*. 26, (1935).

Merkhofer, B. E. 'College Students' Study Behaviour'. Doctoral Thesis, University of Chicago, 1954. (unpublished).

Nedelsky, L. *Science Teaching and Testing*. New York: Harcourt, Brace and World, 1965.

New Zealand Department of Education. *Science for Form V*. Wellington, 1968.

Parkyn, G. W. *Success and Failure at the University*. Vol. 1. Wellington: NZCER, 1959.

Pedley, R. *The Comprehensive School*. Harmondsworth: Penguin Books, 1963.

Peterson, A. D. C. *Arts and Science Sides in the Sixth Form*. Abingdon: Abbey Press, 1960.

Piaget, J. *The Psychology of Intelligence*. London: Routledge and Kegan Paul, 1950.

Plowman, L. and J. B. Stroud. 'The Effect of Informing Pupils of the Correctness of their Responses to Objective Test Questions', *Journal of Educational Research*. 36, (1942).

Rogers, C. A. *Measuring Intelligence in New Zealand*. Auckland: University of Auckland, 1956.

Rosenthal, R., and L. F. Jacobson. 'Teacher Expectations for the Disadvantaged', *Scientific American*. Vol. 218, No. 4, (1968).

Ross, C. C., and L. K. Henry. 'The Relation Between Frequency of Testing and Progress in Learning Psychology', *Journal of Educational Psychology*. 30, (1939).

Stone, G. R. 'The Training Function of Examinations, *U.S.A.F. Training Report*. No. AFPTRC—TN—55—8, (1955).

Stovall, J. F. 'Lecture Versus Discussion', *Phi Delta Kappan*. 39, (1958).

Sutch, W. B. 'Plans Without Planning', 'The J. T. Stewart Lecture on Planning', Palmerston North, 1967. (unpublished).

Svenson, N. E. *Ability Grouping and Scholastic Achievement*. Stockholm: Stockholm Studies in Educational Psychology, 1962.

Tyler, R. W. *Constructing Achievement Tests*. Columbus: Ohio State University Press, 1934.
Tyler, R. W. *Trends in Student Personnel Work*. Minneapolis: University of Minnesota Press, 1949.
University of London Goldsmith's College. *Second Pilot Course for Experienced Teachers*. 1965.
Walbesser, H. H. 'Curriculum Evaluation by Means of Behavioural Objectives', *Journal of Research in Science Teaching*. No. 1. (1963).
Walbesser, H. H. 'Science Curriculum Evaluation', *Science Teacher* (Feb. 1966).

Index

A
ability courses, 29
ability groups *see* class groupings
achievement, importance to child, 13-14
achievement tests, 93-4
Adams, G. S., 91; 92
adolescents, 6; needs recognised, 21-2; potential contributions to society, 58
Aitkin, J. M., 87
All India Council for Education, 90
art, relation to philosophy, 35-6
attainment as basis for grouping, 19
attitudes *see* interests and attitudes

B
behaviour, measurement of changes, 44-5
behaviour type courses, 30
Bellack, A., 100-1
Bloom, Benjamin S., 28; 86; 87; 90; *Taxonomy of Educational Objectives*, 26; 41; 98
Brian, G. L., 90
Bruner, J. S., 28; *Toward a Theory of Instruction*, 82-3; 87; 88-9; 100; *The Process of Education*, 87; *A Study of Thinking*, 89

C
cheating, 13
'child-centred' curricula, 11
children in new towns, 4
church, influence on family life, 5
class groupings, 16-19; criteria for judging, 17-18
class tutors, 58-9
classification of goals, 41
classrooms, need for new concepts, 16
co-education, 8
Commission on Education in New Zealand, 1962. *Report,* 94-5
communications, role in changing society, 2

community and schools, 74-9
competition, dangers in education, 12-14; 30; 75-6
conformity, 21-2
content courses, 29
Council for Educational Research, 81
Cronbach, J., *Educational Psychology*, 81; 82; 91; *Essentials of Psychological Testing*, 93
curriculum, bases for judgement, xiii; 1; role in helping migrant children to adjust, 4; challenged by growth of knowledge, 7-8; teacher's role in developing, 15-16; 42-3; 61-3; 69-70; and class groupings, 19; designed to stimulate enquiry, 36-9; examined in the light of educational aims, 57-73; organisation, 65-7; *see also* content courses; ability courses; behaviour-type courses; enquiry-centred courses
curriculum, child-centred *see* 'child-centred' curricula
Curriculum Development Unit, 81
Curriculum Review Group *see* New Zealand Post-Primary Teachers' Association. Curriculum Review Group

D
Dawson, M. D., 86-7
debate *see* discussion
democratic procedures in schools, 21
desire to learn, 11
discipline approach to learning, 101-2
disciplines, structure, 61-2
discussion, its use in teaching, 27-8; 31; 57-9; 76-7; topics, 98-100
Douglas, H. R., 90
Dressel, P. L., 89; 91

E
economic conditions, influence on education, 3

INDEX

education, role in growth of child, xiii-iv; 1-3; 5-6; 7; 10; basic aims, xi; 1; 10-14; 57; 80-1; changes since Thomas Report, 8; relation to experience, 57-9; and future needs of youth, 74
education, vocational, 67-8
Educational Testing Service, 93
Elley, W. B., 89; 90
emotionally disturbed children, 80
empirical and non-empirical disciplines, 33-8; 64-7
enquiry-centred courses, 30-8
examinations, syllabus revisions, xi; 8; objectives defined, 40-1; limitations in present system, 41-2; potential values, 42-6; external, 46-7; 76; effects on pupils and teachers, 90-5
experience, common, 86
external examinations *see* examinations, external

F
family, changes in role, 4-6
field-trips, 76-7
Fitch, M.L., 90; 91
Flynn, H. E., 87-8; 91
free periods, value to younger pupils, 16
Foshay, A. W., 100
Furst, E. J., 89; 91

G
Gagné, R. M., 87
Galbraith, J. K., *The Affluent Society*, 82
Goldsmith's College *see* University of London. Goldsmith's College
Grey Walter, W., *The Living Brain*, 87
Guetzkow, H., 90

H
Havighurst, R., 103
Hawkes, H. E., 93
Heisenberg, W., 88
Henry, L. K., 91
Hiler, W., 90

Hillmorton High School, 85
Hume, D., 89

I
intellectual growth and social attitudes, 53-4
intelligence, complexity of its nature, 28-9
interests and attitudes, 96-7; ways of measuring, 47-53; relationship to intellect, 53-4

J
Jacobson, L. F., 83-4
Jones, H. E., 90

K
Keislar, E. R., 91
Kirkpatrick, I. E., 91
'knowledge explosion', 7
Kooker, E. W., 91
Kowitz, G. T., 101
Krathwohl, D. R., 49; 52; 53

L
La Fountaine, M. E., *Continuous Learning*, 81-2
learning, definition, 40; and experience, 26-8; and enquiry, 26-39; 67
learning resources, 15; 32; 68-9
liaison officers, 77
Likert Scale, 97
Lumsdaine, A. A., 90

M
McDonald, A., 83
McKeachnie, W. J., 86; 90
Maize, R. C., 90
Maoris, 4; 80
maturity, development through education, 10
mass media, effects on children, 6-7; role in fostering school-community understanding, 75-6
May, M. A., 90
Merkhofer, B.E., 90
Meyer, G., 90

mobility, social, 4
motivation for learning, 10-12; for taking examinations, 45-6
Munro, R. G., 87-8; 91; appointed chairman of the Curriculum Review Group, xi

N

Nedelsky, Leo, 86-7; *Science Teaching and Testing*, 40; 85; 88; 96
New Zealand Department of Education, *Science for Form V*, 92-3
New Zealand Federated Farmers, 101
New Zealand Post-Primary Teachers' Association, Annual Conference, 1966, xi; Curriculum Review Group set up, xi

O

opportunities for learning, 63-9
Otumoetai College, 85

P

Pacific Islanders, 4; 80
parents, role in education, 74-5; 77-8
Pedley, Robin, *The Comprehensive School*, 81
personality adjustment, 97-8
Peterson, A. D. C., 89
philosophical questions, 35-6; 89
philosophy, relation to art, 35-6
Piaget, J., 28; 87
Plowman, L., 91
Post-Primary School Curriculum see Thomas Committee Report
prefects, role in guiding younger children, 20-1
private study, 16
problem solving, 62-3
psychological needs and the curriculum, 60
pulp magazines *see* mass media
punishment, 10-11

R

radio *see* mass media
Rigney, J. W., 90
Rogers, C. A., 87

Rosenthal, R., 83-4
Ross, C. C., 91

S

school certificate, amendments, xi; 19; new science syllabus, 49; evaluated by Commission on Education in New Zealand, 94-5
school councils, 20-1
school experience related to life, 57-8
schools, and the community, 74-9
see also education; co-education
science, influence on society, 7
secondary education *see* education
seminars, teacher-parents, 74-5
skills, variety and development, 28-9
slow learners, 17; 80
Smith, B. P. F., 85-6
social attitudes in children, development by education, 47-54; relation to intellectual development, 53-4
society, predicted changes, 2-9
specialists as visitors to schools, 76-7
Stone, G. R., 90
Storall, J. F., 86
streaming *see* class groupings
Stroud, J. B., 91
Sutch, W. B., 101
Svenson, Nils Eric, *Ability Grouping and Scholastic Achievement*, 84
Sweden, experiments with unstreamed classes, 18

T

Tallmadge, M., 90
teachers, training, xi; 8; relations with pupils, 11-12; 14-15; 20; 31; role in developing new curricula, 15-16; 42-3; 61-3; 69-70; team approach, 59; co-operation with parents, 74-5; 77-8
teaching aids *see* learning resources
technology, influence on society, 7
television *see* mass media
tests *see* examinations
textbooks, 31-2
Thomas Committee, 1942, xi; Report, 8

Thurston Scale, 97
Timaru Girls' High School, 85
transport *see* communications
Tyler, R. W., 89; 91

U
University Entrance Examination, xi; 94
University of London, Goldsmith's College, *First Pilot Course for Experienced Teachers*, 102; *Second Pilot Course for Experienced Teachers*, 103

V
vocational education *see* education, vocational
Volunteer Service Abroad, 2

W
Waihi College, 85
Walbesser, H. H., 87
Westlake Girls' High School, 85
Williams, C. S., 91
women, changing role in family, 5